D0871911

# Mindful

# HORSEMANSHIP

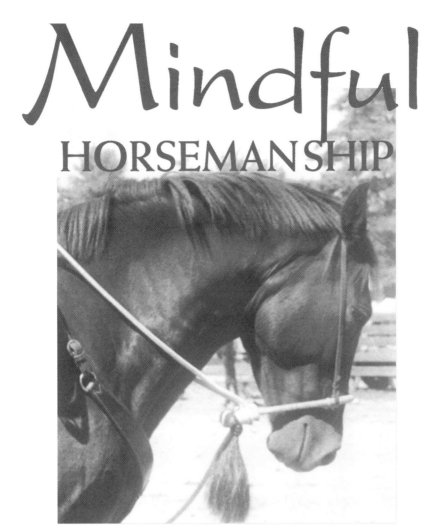

**INCREASING YOUR AWARENESS**

**ONE DAY AT A TIME**

Cheryl Kimball

CARRIAGE HOUSE PUBLISHING
Middleton, New Hampshire

First published in 2002 by Carriage House Publishing Company.
Copyright 2002 by Cheryl Kimball

Cover photo of Andrea Morgan's horse "Kiwi" by Kelly Blake
Cover and interior design by Eliot House Productions
Printed in China through World Print, Ltd.

Carriage House Publishing books are available at a discount in bulk quantities for promotional uses. For details about special sales, contact the publisher.

Carriage House Publishing
223 Silver Street
Middleton, NH 03887
603-755-4596

ISBN 0-9670047-1-3

Library of Congress Cataloging-in-Publication Data Available

*To Frannie*

*Her generosity and kindness is unmatched.*
*She is a mentor and a friend*
*in the truest sense of the word.*

# ACKNOWLEDGMENTS

Special thanks to Bud, the horse who got me into all this. He was two when I bought him, he is 13 at this writing, and he continues to be a puzzle to me. Bud is such an interesting horse that he keeps me going back to the classroom to see if I can make one tiny step more in his direction.

Thanks a million to Stephanie Levy for turning her expert eye to this before I committed it to print. She is an inspiration in her work ethic and her ability with horses.

Thanks, as always, to Jack, man-who-sings-to-the-animals, and who listens to more long orations about horses than any non-rider should have to.

And, of course, thanks to everyone whose words of wisdom comprise this book but especially to the clinicians with whom I have had the privilege of studying. I would like to particularly thank Buck Brannaman, who drives all the way to the east coast every year to continue what he started back in 1991, and to his family who is without him much of the year so he can travel and help the rest of us. Buck's first clinic at Piper Ridge Farm in Limerick, Maine, started a new chapter for me and my life with horses. That's one book I hope to never finish.

*Mindful horsemanship is not a destination but a manner of traveling.*

—me

Mindfulness has many definitions; "living in the moment" is perhaps the best way to describe this concept. Most animals except humans live in the moment, making mindfulness a way of life for them. Mindfulness plays a key role in Zen Buddhism—learning, through meditation and other practices such as martial arts, archery, and flower arranging, to clear the mind of the clouds of useless thought in order to live more fully in the present.

But the definition of mindfulness I think of the most when it comes to my interaction with horses is the concept of "being aware." I associate mindfulness with my grandmother's era; along with saying "Hark!" when she wanted me to be quiet and listen, she might have cautioned me to "be mindful of the stairs."

The British subway system has given me one of my favorite phrases, "mind the gap," which is announced with regularity to alert passengers to the space between the platform and the train.

Look around you. *See* things. Be aware. I have come to believe in my ten-plus years of trying to develop my own good horsemanship abilities that awareness is the key.

If you increase your awareness, you can perfect your timing—simply by being aware of your actions and the horse's response. If you increase your awareness, you can perfect your balance—by being aware of your own position and movements. If you increase your awareness, you can begin to accomplish the fine and elusive concept of "feel."

When it comes to interacting with horses, awareness and feel are almost synonyms, I think. When you begin teaching a horse to lead with feel (really what you are doing is teaching yourself to lead the horse while allowing the horse to retain her innate high level of sensitivity but that's a long story), you pick up on your horse's lead rope and ask her to step ahead; when she begins to move, you will be aware enough to release the lead rope for that movement at the exact moment when that release means something to her. When you crank your awareness up a notch, you will begin to release when the horse hasn't actually moved but merely shifted her weight. What comes next may be the point where awareness and feel part ways—you can develop your awareness to the point where you can begin to know when the horse has just *thought* about leading ahead, then you release. At this level of refinement your request and release become something quite different, not a request and release at all but simply working together. This is where you begin to build toward an extremely fine-tuned relationship with an extremely sensitive animal.

It is this relationship that this book is about—a relationship built through developing your awareness, and therefore your ability to communicate with your horse. That awareness and communication skill is developed through an attitude that over-lays everything you do at first in relation to horses, and eventually in relation to life in general. Please don't get me wrong, I am in no way suggesting by writing this book that I think I am "there." Far from it! But as the quote above says (which is anony-mous and originally said "happiness" but I altered it for my own purposes), mindful horsemanship is not an endpoint to work toward, but a way of being to work within.

The path to awareness is what keeps me going to clinics again and again—to be reminded of where I need to be more aware in my interactions with my horses. At some point in the past few years, this "manner of traveling" became ingrained enough in me that I began to relate information and advice in everything I read and heard—from equine writers to horse clinicians to concentration camp survivor and world-renowned logotherapist Viktor Frankl to controversial novelist Ayn Rand and even Pooh's Eeyore—to my attempt at understanding horses. I hope my own mental meanderings from these diverse jumping off points provide inspiration for you—not only to carry on in a long process that can be supremely frustrating at the same time it is supremely rewarding, but also to develop your own thinking and questioning and ultimately your own personal mindful philosophy within the larger scope of communicating with horses.

—Cheryl Kimball

*Mindful practice, in its purest sense, is simply this: be aware of what is, what is here in the moment.*

—Charles T. Tart
in *Living the Mindful Life*

Mindfulness doesn't seem to be innate for humans. I guess it is our unique ability to self-analyze and project into the future that interferes with our ability to be totally in the present. It may be a lifelong process, but if we can start with being mindful while we are riding and working with our horses, we may find a head start on being mindful in the rest of our lives and we certainly will find working with our horses will be greatly affected.

*Awareness takes you beyond the mechanics of your riding.*

—from *Beyond the Mirrors*
by Jill Keiser Hassler

A lot of people focus intently on riding mechanics. They develop into "perfect" riders and support the horse just by the mechanics of staying in their seat, good balance, and quiet legs and hands. This is important for competitors since appearance is so critical in the competitive world. But these masters of equitation often seem to be lacking something. That something is feel.

Before I ever learned about the mechanics of a car, I needed to develop a feel for driving. Once I had a feel for driving, I began to care how the car was operating—if it seemed like the engine was skipping, the tires were low, or other mechanical fine tuning.

If you develop awareness and feel, mechanics will readily follow.

*A thing "takes as long as it takes."*

—from *Self Defense for Women*
by Liz Pennell

Working with horses, especially educating young horses, is best done without time limits. Once you start something, you should plan to finish it. If you can't finish it, at the very least end on a positive, learning note, not a sour note where you and your horse came to an impasse and you needed to stop because your friends were expecting you at the bowling lanes by 7:00.

And likewise, in a more general sense, it may take three years to get your horse to feel comfortable with a specific thing you want her to do. There are many specific things to work on to get there—straightness of the horse, balance of the rider—but unless you are under the constraints of competition it is really not significant how long it takes for all the pieces to come together.

*Speak or act with an impure mind
and trouble will follow you...
Speak or act with a pure mind
and happiness will follow you,
as your shadow, unshakable.*

—Buddha (Siddhartha Gautama,
founder of Buddhism)

Horses size humans up pretty quickly. If you ask for something and don't mean it, the horse knows and trouble will surely follow. If you are acting in a way that you do not truly feel, the horse knows it. I've seen people buy a piece of equipment that they see a good horseman using at a clinic—a rope halter or a particular snaffle bit for instance—and think that now that they are using this instead of a nose chain or a curb bit or whatever they had been using that they instantly are practicing good horsemanship. It isn't just about equipment, it is what thought process is going through your entire body. With pure thoughts and pure actions, good horsemanship is yours.

*It's actually quite good discipline to be kept away
from it. It builds up all sorts of ideas and urges.*

—from *The Pleasing Hour*
by Lily King

The "it" being discussed in this quote is sculpture. But the quote can apply to anything you practice to get better at. Have you ever attended a clinic just to watch and ten minutes into the first class, you wished you were riding your horse?

When I joined a mentoring program for pre-teens, my horse friends thought I would make it a criteria to be matched with a kid who loves horses. But in fact, I was just as happy to spend time doing non-horse-related things. Getting away from what absorbs you can help keep you fresh.

*I found my first fossil bone, I think,*
*in 1950 at the age of six...*
*I became engrossed and was soon entirely oblivious of*
*the heat and flies for the first time that day.*

—Richard Leakey,
archaeologist

When something truly interests you, you don't notice things like heat and flies. And the same is true for the horse, especially young horses—if you keep your horse busy and interested enough in what you are doing, the horse will forget about being cranky and get involved in what you are doing. It's a key part of focus, being engrossed in something that has been made interesting to you.

*"There's two sides to a horse and what you got to do is work the one side and let the other side go."*

*"You don't think you could train both sides of the horse the same?"*

*"But what would you have when you got done?"*

*"You'd have a two-sided, balanced horse."*

—from *Cities of the Plain*
by Cormac McCarthy

J have heard it said that because of the position of the horse's eye, the horse's left side experiences a completely different world than her right side. And you do need to address both sides of the horse—sacking her out on the left and right, lead her on both sides, even mount and dismount on the so-called "off" side once in a while! If you pay enough attention to both sides you get, as McCarthy's character John Grady Cole says here, a "two-sided, balanced horse."

*If you don't risk anything, you risk even more.*

—Erica Jong,
writer

You can't always "play it safe" with horses. Although you can stack the deck heavily in your favor by educating your horse properly and thoroughly, at some point you do need to get your horse exposed to the world, to new things and new ideas. There's nothing like the experience of the trail itself, but you can increase your odds of success on the trail by simulating some things in a safe place like a round pen. I have found that even more than those kinds of activities, the key to being comfortable exposing your horse to new things is to have some tools to draw on when something comes up—to be able to place your horse's feet where you need them so you can maneuver a tough spot on the trail, work on straightness so you can get through a tight spot without taking your knee off on a gatepost, those kinds of things.

*Let no one ever come to you without leaving better
and happier.*

—Mother Theresa

This attitude seems like one that is as good to apply to horses
as to people.

*I don't know a whole lot about geese. Maybe it's ok for them to grow up thinking they're airplanes... But with a horse, I reckon first you have to let them learn to be a horse.*

—from *The Horse Whisperer*
by Nicholas Evans

J bought a two-year-old filly who had been an "only horse." She had been well cared for and had a nice home, but she had not learned much about being a horse. When she came to my place, my mare and gelding began to teach her some signals that she should pay attention to. But it took quite a bit of bossing around by them and a more drastic incident with an older mare who was visiting for a few weeks before my filly really learned how to interact with other horses. Luckily she was not badly hurt and the result seemed to be that instead of having to actually be bitten or chased by one of the older horses, she now can recognize a signal from afar.

*In the absence of certainty, instinct is all you can follow.*

—Jonathan Cainer

You can increase the likelihood of your instincts being accurate by getting as much knowledge as you can. But using your instincts and trying something, even if it turns out not to be the "right" thing is usually better than doing nothing at all.

*If they leave from the front first, then they are just dragging the back along.*

—Tom Curtin,
horseman

J found this an interesting concept and one that I have tried to think more about as I work with my horses. It makes sense, considering the horse's impulsion comes from the hindquarters. But the thing that interests me the most about the quote is how important it is to constantly think about and try to understand the movement of the horse and how it affects everything you do with them.

*When the student is ready, the teacher will appear.*

—Anonymous

When I bought an unstarted 2-year-old gelding as my re-entry into the horse world after a 13-year hiatus, I knew I had to teach the horse some things but I didn't yet know that I was the one more in need of a teacher. This big strong horse would drag me down the driveway when I took him for "walks" and run into the corner of the corral and kick at me with both feet when I lunged him. An incident with a farrier made me realize I couldn't to send him to a "horse trainer" and just when I was at my wit's end about what to do, I read about an upcoming Buck Brannaman clinic nearby. I visited the farm where the clinic was to be held to find out more information and when I left, although I didn't realize it yet, I had found my teachers.

*In the course of an hour with their horse, most people spend 40 minutes somewhere else and the other 20 they're mad. And they wonder why things aren't going right with their horse.*

—Tom McDowell, horse trainer,
in an interview

Being mad is going to get you nowhere with your horse, and it may get you somewhere worse than that. Horses don't do things to get humans mad, although that may be the result of their actions. If you can get beyond being mad about the way things are or aren't going when you are working with your horse, leave anger completely out of the picture, and instead react to each thing as a learning experience for both of you, you will have a lot more pleasant time with your horse!

*Our actions are our only true belongings.*

—Thich Nhat Hanh,
spiritual leader

$S$ince the explosion in popularity of so-called "natural horse-manship clinics," many people have labeled themselves clinicians and sought their fortune traveling the country showing people how to communicate with horses. It is often difficult to assess the quality of these clinicians, but you definitely don't want to rely on glossy brochures, words in books, and sophisticated websites. Go see clinicians interact with horses. Their actions, and more important the horses' reactions to the clinicians will tell you all you need to know.

*Watch [the left fielder's] feet as the pitcher accepts the
sign and gets ready to pitch. A good left fielder knows
what pitch is coming, and he can tell from the angle of
the bat where the ball is going to be hit. . .*

—from *Shoeless Joe*
by W.P. Kinsella

The first time I saw clinician Buck Brannaman, I thought he
was some sort of magician. As he was working a horse in a
round pen, he would point out what it was going to do next,
and the horse would do it. I kept looking for the invisible lines
connecting him and the horse that allowed him to move the
horse, marionette-like, to make his predictions come true. Of
course, his "invisible lines" actually consisted of the ability to
read the horse's finest movements and positions.

To do this you need to become aware of "what happened
before what happened happened," to quote Ray Hunt—how the
way the horse is standing affects how he is going to move next,
how the horse is traveling has an impact on what is physically
possible for the horse to do for its next move. It's like Shoeless
Joe—he learned how to read the bat in order to anticipate the
ball's movement before the ball was actually struck. So someone
could look at Shoeless Joe's feet and predict which way he is
positioning himself to move to know where the ball would go.

*You should know, before you attempt to do anything,*
*just what you are going to do, and how you are going to*
*do it.*

—from *The Modern Art of Taming Wild Horses*
by J.S. Rarey

Make a plan so you have a place to start and perhaps a place to finish, but if things don't go along as planned be flexible! Adjust to fit the horse and where she is at. Maybe the lesson you had planned for today isn't the lesson she needs today or maybe it's just the way you planned to teach the lesson that isn't working for the horse. If you were headed to the movies and the road you usually take is closed for repairs, you wouldn't abandon your plan to go to the movies, but would instead either take another road or go to another movie theatre. Think about alternate routes with your horse too, and have some creative ideas up your sleeve for when things aren't going as planned.

*Every horse is different, just like every man is different.*
*With enough experience, both the horse and the man*
*will learn to anticipate what each other needs.*

—from *The Forgotten Arts Book 3*,
quote by Cliff Peasley

We don't want to strive to have our horses anticipate what we want so much that we make them act without thinking. What we do strive for is to have our horses understand the slightest request, and we to understand their slightest try to accomplish what we have asked of them.

As you start to be extra mindful of the way you handle your horses, see if there isn't some specific thing that you could work on to become more consistent, whether it's leading, backing, or picking up a foot. Recognize your horse's slightest try. Build on both your consistency and the horse's attempts and you will be amazed how quickly things fall together.

*Horses and life, it's all the same to me.*

—Buck Brannaman,
horseman

Buck's life with horses is a bit more extreme than most of us, since he works with hundreds of horses each year. So in a very real sense, horses are his life. But this quote is reaching beyond that surface interpretation. When you get interested in refining your relationship with your horse, this thought resonates even with us backyard horse owners. Horses move from being a novelty or even a pet, to just being a part of life.

*If you don't know where you are going, you will probably end up somewhere else.*

—Lawrence J. Peter

You need to have a goal in order to get where you want to be. You may end up somewhere else anyway, but you'll never end up at your goal if you don't have one.

*When I put myself in a cow's place, I really have to be that cow and not a person in a cow's costume. I place myself inside its body and imagine what it experiences.*

—from *Thinking In Pictures*
by Temple Grandin

Temple Grandin is autistic and uses her unique abilities in unique perspective in the cattle industry. She is not anthropomorphizing here—she is not suggesting that what the cow thinks and how it reacts is the way a human would think and react.

When I owned sheep, people often said to me that they have heard that sheep are incredibly stupid. My response was that sheep think like sheep, and make sheep choices, and these choices often may not seem to be the best ones in the eyes of the human.

We need to think about how the horse thinks and reacts, respect that, and help the horse learn to react in new ways that are more fitting with the human/horse relationship. If we want our horses basically to shun millions of years of evolution for our sake, we need in return to give the horse reason to have some supreme confidence in us.

*Experience is the worst kind of teacher. It gives you the test first, and the lesson afterward.*

—Unknown

Experience is the key way to develop your communication skills with horses, and with horses you often have to learn some ways to stay as safe as possible and then just dig in there.

When I bought a two-year-old gelding after not being around horses for quite a few years, I kept him for the first couple years in boarding stables. It wasn't until I finally owned a place where I could have my horse in my own yard and began to get day-to-day interaction with horses that I felt I could push to the next level of communication with them.

*...no animal can be trained by fear.*

—from *Atlas Shrugged*
by Ayn Rand

When you are handling a thousand-pound animal, fear seems like it would be the worst place to have that animal working from. Unless there is mutual respect, some day, some how, a horse's instinct for self preservation from what it fears is going to surface. It has to—the horse is programmed for self protection at all costs.

Although some of it has changed as their customers' expectations have changed, the horse training world has largely built its reputation on training by fear and intimidation—spurs are used as punishment not motivators. The horse is always afraid of what may happen if it doesn't do the "right" thing. Some horses get along and can go through the whole training process, others fall apart. The ones who don't fall apart learn to operate in a very mechanical matter, never assuming it is ok for them to think something through. When self-preservation kicks in with these horses, it is often long after the trainer is no longer part of the picture since the ones with a high level of self-preservation don't make it to the show circuit, are sold a couple times, and end up in the hands of novices who become the brunt of the actions of a horse who has been trained to be fearful of humans—and the pair often end up at a clinic together as the last resort. This vicious cycle is beginning to be broken and there are many "horse trainers" who are looking at horses differently and are willing, and in fact insist, that the owner be part of the process.

*Knowledge is not reality.*
*Experience belongs to the past...*

—Yosano Akiko,
poet

We often think that knowledge and experience are all we can draw on; however, we need to be ever mindful of the present. Horses live in the here and now, and occasionally what is happening right now is all the knowledge and experience we have to draw on. And it might also be all we need. Horse people often like to recap a ride like a bunch of bridge players going over the last game. This just bogs you down, focus on this ride.

*We can do anything we want if we stick to it long enough.*

—Helen Keller,
deaf and blind lecturer

With horses, the hard part about sticking to it long enough is not drilling our horses on something. But if we keep trying to find new ways to approach something, instead of asking the horse to change, and give the new approach long enough, we will get done what we wanted to get done. It may not be today, it may not be tomorrow, but it will be whatever amount of time is long enough.

*The two horses came up close to me, looking with great earnestness upon my face and hands.... Upon the whole, the behavior of these animals was so orderly and rational, so acute and judicious, that I at last concluded they must needs be magicians.*

—from *Gulliver's Travels*
by Jonathan Swift

The thought of horses being magicians makes me smile! I particularly liked Swift's recognition of some special quality that the horse has.

*Until those feet move where you need them, the horse is going to be where he is.*

—from *True Unity*
by Tom Dorrance

Unless the feet move under your direction, even if the horse moves he is where *he* is, not where you put him. Being mindful of the horse's feet at all times and learning how to direct them is perhaps the most important way to advance your horsemanship—both on the ground and in the saddle.

*The body says what words cannot.*

—Martha Graham,
dancer, choreographer

For the horse, the body is everything. They speak with their bodies, of course, since words are not within their grasp. What they read from our bodies can be amazing—we see it all the time when we watch an advanced rider changing gaits with her or his horse with requests that are invisible to our eyes.

A group of clinic goers in my area get together every other Sunday throughout the winter for what we have referred to as The Winter Riding Club. Each time, one of the group is responsible for coming up with the day's lesson. One week, we invited a woman who gives lessons and is a good equitation teacher. She worked with all of us on making the transition from the trot to the canter by becoming aware of our body rhythm and using it to change the horse's gait. At the trot, we are in the 1-2, 1-2, 1-2 rhythm of the horse's steps. To get to the canter, moving your body's rhythm to the 1-2-3, 1-2-3, 1-2-3 of the horse's cantering beat will quickly get your horse to change its gait to get into time with your body. It is an interesting exercise and often the horse gets it a lot faster than the human!

Since words are not too useful for horses, we can move our communication up a notch by becoming aware of the language of our bodies.

*Anxiety impairs the ability to think.*

—from *Extraordinary Relationships*
by Roberta Gilbert

Gilbert was speaking of humans here, but she could have been speaking of any animal. Even though horses cannot have the same mental capabilities of the human, they have a brain and a mind and a heart and therefore the ability to feel anxious. And perhaps their anxiety is even greater than the humans because of the fact that they cannot interpret the depth of their experience the way humans can.

Horses react to anxiety in horselike ways, which means that if we try to teach the horse something by using force, the horse will become fearful or resentful; many will respond in a defensive manner to what it perceives as a threat, others will simply always exhibit an anxiousness, like the horse who is constantly on the edge waiting for a spur in the side.

Be mindful of the subtle ways that your horse tells you it is anxious. Don't ignore this anxiety, respect it. Help your horse through these anxious spots in whatever way works for you and the horse. Some people use verbal praise, some people simply try to communicate confidence to the horse to help them be confident, some people use other more mechanical means like a clicker or treats. Whatever you use, don't ignore the anxiety your horse feels or expect the horse to simply ignore its anxious feelings.

*You can be sure that there will be problems in the training of your horse, both during ground schooling and during mounted work, because that is what training is all about.*

—from *The Hackamore Reinsman*
by Ed Connell

J prefer the concept of "teaching" rather than "training." And, as with humans, I feel we are teaching our horses throughout their entire lives, not just in that 90-day period after they are first started under saddle. And with that ongoing teaching comes, as Ed Connell says, ongoing "problems."

To be able to communicate with a horse leads to being able to teach them something. It is knowing that you can communicate, that you can break something down enough to teach it to the horse that allows you to be able to embrace the "problems." Problems are simply an opportunity to teach. As long as we don't let problems escalate to the point of being dangerous, we can look at them with a gleam in our eye as an opportunity to move one rung higher on the ladder of communication with our horses.

*It takes one act of manipulation, arrogance,
insensitivity, or dishonesty to destroy what it may
have taken years to build in a relationship.*

—from *Near-Life Experiences*
by Tom McQueen

Horses are very sensitive animals who can sense manipulation, arrogance, insensitivity, and dishonesty and will act accordingly. But horses are also very forgiving animals; making "mistakes" may set back your relationship a notch or two, but it will not destroy trust if that relationship has been built on honesty and good intentions.

*On horseback, he seemed to require as many hands as a
Hindu god, at least four for clutching the reins, and two
more for patting the horse soothingly on the neck.*

—H. H. Munro (Saki),
writer

*O*ften this is what it feels like when you're trying to handle
the reins and support your horse with a pat or two at crucial
moments. Add a lariat to it, and it's really a trick! That's why it
can be best to try new things—like working with a rope—in a
controlled, safe environment like a good round pen. The last
thing you want is to have to abandon supporting your horse; in
a round pen or arena you can keep patting and choose to abandon your reins instead.

*Our answer must consist not in talk and medication,*
*but in right action and in right conduct.*

—Viktor Frankl,
psychologist

Your actions are what mean the most to your horse. I ride a lot with a friend who is interested in alternative treatments. She knew my young mare had difficulty when we had to pass a house where two large dogs always came charging out to the end of the driveway. I knew the dogs were contained with an invisible fence but my mare, of course, didn't understand that. The next time we rode that way, my friend brought along a Bach flower remedy that is said to "instill courage." I agreed with my friend that it was courage my horse needed to gain, but I wanted her courage to come from her trust in me. A source like flower essences would hold no meaning for her, the courage would essentially be given to her not achieved by her (and me). I enjoy the process of working through these things as much if not more than the end result.

*You don't have to be strong to control a horse, you just
need to know what to control.*

—Chris Cox, clinician,
at a clinic

Although strength, in my opinion, cannot be dismissed all
together, if you learn to direct your horse's feet then strength is
certainly a lot less of an issue. When your horse knows to move
in a certain direction when you do a certain thing then you can
keep yourself out of danger without needing to be strong. For
instance, when I have my horse on a lead rope and I take the
slack out of the lead and bring her head slightly to the left and
step in toward her left hip, she moves her hindquarters to the
right. So, if she is acting up for whatever reason or decides she
needs to threaten something with her hind feet, I can use this
same move to get her to swing her hindquarters away. I may
have to be quick but I don't have to be strong! It all boils down
to the feet.

*To know oneself is to study oneself in action with another person.*

—from *Tao of Jeet Kune Do*
by Bruce Lee

The same could be said of studying oneself in action with a horse. Some people have had to learn to be completely different in order to be successful in interacting with horses. And not only is it important to learn the most fitting way to interact with horses in general, but if you study your actions you can learn what worked with a particular horse and what didn't.

*Mistakes are part of the dues one pays for a full life.*

—Sophia Loren,
actor

Ah, there's that word again, "mistakes." While it's important not to get hung up on mistakes, sometimes we do things that simply are mistakes! I know I've apologized to my new colt several times in his short life here at my place for making one move more than I should have, i.e., a "mistake." But he seems to forgive me pretty fast.

You can either lock yourself in a closet and live a pretty boring life or you can put yourself out there on the line and live a full life that includes a few mistakes. Choose the latter, your horse will forgive you.

*Everlasting happiness is an inner state that doesn't depend on favorable external circumstances.*

—from *Open Mind*
by Diane Mariechild

I once went on a house tour that included a farm with a horse barn that had stalls with stained glass windows in the doors. The building was beautiful and made the home look magazine-perfect but the environment was created with people in mind, not horses. Nutritious food, fresh water, freedom of movement, and quality handling make a horse much happier than any fancy building.

*It seems silly to me to debate over whether or not
animals can think. To me it has always been obvious
that they do.*

—from *Thinking in Pictures*
by Temple Grandin

Believe it or not, there are people who do not believe a horse
can think. And then there are people who do not give the horse
the option to think. A horse is a living creature with a brain and
it does think. Simple as that. Horses thoughts may not be as
complex as human thoughts but this does not make their
thought process any less important to them than ours is to us.

*When I came back to riding at forty-four, every little two-foot fence looked to me like a Puissance wall.*

—Jane Smiley
in *Horse People*

$\mathcal{I}$ too came back to riding as an adult, and I'm sure a lot of people can probably relate to this quote. It seems best for you and your horse if you are realistic about your fears and things that you are no longer comfortable with.

I recently started my third young horse under saddle. My first—ten years ago—was a minor disaster, my second effort went well and instilled great confidence in me. These two different experiences made me realize that I would be doing my latest filly a favor by having the best rider possible take that first ride on her. I am lucky enough to live only thirty miles from a facility that hosts clinics by some of the best horsemen in the world, so I had one of these clinicians take that first ride on my filly. I did all the preparation—the best halter breaking job I could, the first saddling—so that the clinician could focus on riding. After he gave her that first supportive ride and she accepted the ride calmly, I took over riding her for the rest of the clinic.

*My true religion is kindness.*

—Dalai Lama,
religious leader

Kindness doesn't cost anything and offering kindness to a horse is the cheapest thing you can contribute to your horse's well being. But don't mistake spoiling your horse for being kind to it. Spoiling a horse is perhaps among the worst things you can do. A spoiled horse becomes a pain to have around—not to mention dangerous—and when you tire of the antics you have taught it, a spoiled horse is hard to re-educate and hard to sell since few people want to pay good money for someone else's problems.

Learn to be kind to your horse in ways that a horse can appreciate—learn how to pat it, feed it properly, and handle it, and you will both reap the rewards.

*Whenever the horse stopped (which it did very often),*
*he fell off in front; and whenever it went on again*
*(which it generally did rather suddenly), he fell off*
*behind. Otherwise, he kept on pretty well, except that he*
*had a habit of now and then falling off sideways;*
*and as he generally did this on the side on which Alice*
*was walking, she soon found that it was the best plan*
*not to walk* quite *close to the horse.*

—from *Through the Looking Glass*
by Lewis Carroll

Alice did the adjusting here, but better, of course, would be if the rider had done the adjusting and tried to correct whatever it was that he was doing that made him fall off so regularly!

Don't be afraid to do something or try to teach your horse something because you might do it wrong. The horse will let you know if you made a mistake, and if you're intentions are good, the horse is a very forgiving animal and will do everything it can to try to figure out what you're asking of him.

But if you keep doing the same thing over and over even though you aren't getting the results you want, don't expect the horse to adjust when you aren't doing any adjusting yourself.

*The main thing is, every morning when I wake up,*
*I go do something I really enjoy. How many people in*
*the world can say that?*

—Tiger Woods,
professional golfer

When I first got back into horses, I had a gelding that was way beyond my skill level. I struggled with him for a few years working to increase my ability to support him. In the meantime I got a six-month-old filly and when I started her under saddle she, unlike my gelding, was willing to fill in for my mistakes. I became so comfortable with her that most of the time I laugh when she "pulls" something, and we work our way through it.

Now when I see friends who are struggling with their horses, I not only empathize with them, but I feel compelled to tell them that it is possible, and important, to have fun with their horses!

We hate to "give up" on our difficult horses but if this is a hobby and not what you do for a living, then you don't want to get burned out by always having struggles with your horse. Ultimately, that doesn't help you or the horse.

*...the constant endeavour to understand the creatures entrusted to my care became the reason why, though I was their trainer, I feel as their pupil today...*

—from *My Horses, My Teachers*
by Alois Podhajsky

When you are with your horses, think about what you are learning from them. Everyday they are teaching you about how to communicate with them. If you are open to it, you will realize that you learn at least as much from them as they learn from you.

*Ships in harbor are safe, but that's not what ships are built for.*

—John Shedd

At some point in your horse life, you need to just venture out and see where you get. "Venturing out" will mean something different to everyone—for one person it may be starting your horse over fences, for others it may be simply riding outside of an arena.

It's certainly important to spend time in the arena or round pen or other "safe" environment until you have at least basic control of the tools you need to be as safe as possible on your horse, but this is not what horses "are built for" and eventually you'll want to move out of your comfort zone. This is where you will make leaps and bounds toward a higher level of communication with your horse.

Until she left my property for a clinic, my Arabian filly had no idea the world was so huge and contained so many horses! At the clinic, I was the only consistent factor for her. She timidly checked out her new surroundings, but she clearly found me to be a comfort to her. My affection for her, and certainly our ability to communicate with each other, was stepped up a notch simply by "venturing out."

———·•·———

*If they are doing something wrong, give them an alternative, something else to do.*

—from a lecture by Carolyn Hock,
New Hampshire SPCA

$S$o many people turn to punishment when a horse does something wrong, but punishment is not the answer—it's always too late, it's not meaningful to the horse, and serves no purpose but to make you feel better at first but eventually to feel worse. The horse simply does not know she is doing something wrong—most of the time she is doing exactly what we are telling her to do and we don't know it. Perhaps we don't think we are telling her to do what she is doing, and therefore we think what she is doing is wrong, but to her it isn't wrong. And when the wrong thing is something like biting, the idea of giving them an alternative to not bite in the first place is exactly what to do.

*If you always approach a horse with respect, and an*
*open mind, he'll be the most reliable teacher*
*you'll ever have.*

—Joe Wolter from "Another Approach"
in *America's Horse*
(Jan/Feb 2000)

Think about the people you consider to be your teachers. They've probably always been people for whom you have respect—the people you put on your most polite behavior for, perhaps those that you call "sir" or "ma'am" or those people you call first when you need some advice.

Before you can learn anything from your horses, you first have to believe that horses have the ability to teach. In order to accept horses as teachers, you need to respect them. If horses are no more than "dumb animals" to a person, that person is certainly not going to be looking to the horse as a teacher.

And horses probably won't teach in typical ways. But that's ok, think about films that have been made out of extraordinary teachers—they are always singled out as using unconventional methods to get their lesson across. Horses will not teach conventionally either—we need to learn to find the lesson.

*It takes considerable knowledge just to realize the extent
of your own ignorance.*

—Thomas Sowell

Ever since I started to get even the most basic grasp of good
horsemanship, I have felt that every door that opens leads to
countless other doors opening, every light bulb that goes off
illuminates countless others still unlit, every tool I come to learn
opens up the endless possibilities that the toolbox holds. So
each piece of knowledge we add to our repertoire carries its own
multiple levels of knowledge. For me it is at once a joy and a
frustration!

*Opportunity dances with those already on the*
*dance floor.*

—H. Jackson Brown Jr.
from *A Hero in Every Heart*

The person who wants a genuine, sincere relationship with a
horse needs to have a genuine, sincere attitude in everything he
or she does. You can't turn these things on and off and expect
these traits to just be there whenever you may need them. You
need to already be "on the dance floor."

*An unhurried sense of time is in itself a form of wealth.*

—Bonnie Freidman

Horses are experts at taking our time constraints and tossing them to the wind. If you have only ten minutes to get your horse in the trailer, you can be sure it will take sixty—unless you've tipped the odds in your favor and have made it a point when time is not a factor to refine all those things that help a horse load in a trailer.

*The horse is God's gift to man.*

—Arabian proverb

With all the layers of complexity that a horse has that makes it an unlikely candidate for successful interaction with humans let alone to carry us on their backs, there certainly must be something to the idea that horses were made for humans—not as our beast of burden but to give us pleasure and make us better people. Perhaps their job on this earth is to make us more introspective, to figure our what within ourselves is making it impossible to accomplish something with a horse—I can't think why else they would put up with my inadequacies!

*...respect children and allow them to learn.*

—from a review of *What to Look for in a Classroom
and Other Essays*

J worked for a number of years for a book publisher that
published books on education, particularly what became known
as "whole language." The term, now a little out of vogue, is
nothing more than a nametag that satisfies the human need to
name things. The tag was used to name an overall philosophy of
teaching that, among other things, puts the student first;
believes that children learn best by being taught in ways that
hold meaning opposed to rote memorization; that every part of
the curriculum—math, science, reading, art—can be intercon-
nected and used to teach the other parts; and that we need to
respect children as individuals with ideas and concerns as much
as we need them to respect adults.

This philosophy resonated with me. As I began to get into
"natural horsemanship" (another misnomer in the human need to
name things), I became fascinated by the parallels it held with
the whole language approach to teaching. Horses deserve to be
respected as thinking, feeling beings. In order for learning to be
thorough, they need to understand the lesson, to have it hold
meaning for them and not just be drilled through conditioned
response. The horse world, like the education world, insisted on
having to put a name to a way of thinking even though it's really
not a "thing" but an attitude.

*What fascinated me about animals was the ready access
they seemed to have to their emotions.*

—from *When Elephants Weep*
by Jeffrey Moussaieff Masson
and Susan McCarthy

Perhaps the strongest emotion horses possess is fear (i.e., self preservation). They get into many situations where they are fearful and therefore spend a lot of time reaching to that emotion. Luckily another strong "emotion" in horses is forgiveness. They allow us to make mistakes and for the most part don't seem to hold grudges.

*A bad-tempered man will never make a good-tempered horse.*

—from *Black Beauty*
by Anna Sewall

During my first clinic, I built up a bit of anger. Some of it was directed toward myself for not knowing how to handle my young horse. Some of it was directed toward my gelding—I was doing the best I could to offer him a good deal, so why did he keep stepping on me, pushing me around, paying attention to everything but me, and just being unpleasant and dangerous in general?

Buck Brannaman was the clinician and he made the comment that he could see that a few of us had a bit of a temper and couldn't he have some fun with that. Well, from that moment on I attempted to get my anger under control. But I didn't fully get over getting angry with a horse until I completely understood that with horses, almost everything relies on the human. Sure, some horses can be easier to deal with than others, but until the human gets more adept at adjusting to fit the horse, the horse will react in ways that test our patience.

*You can talk and listen to horses all you want, and
what you will learn, if you pay close attention, is that
they live on open ground way beyond language...*

—from Bill Dorrance's obituary
by Verlyn Klinkenborg
in *The New York Times*

This is one of my favorite quotes. The idea that horses "live on open ground way beyond language" gets, I think, pretty close to the essence of the horse.

To approach it with a more literal interpretation, I've heard people ask some of the clinicians I've ridden with why they don't "put voice commands" on horses. For one thing, they claim that they don't want someone else to be able to influence their horse while they are riding—most of us have experienced the school horse who we are trotting but the instructor tells a student at the other end of the arena to "walk" and our horse immediately drops to the walk. But the other answer is that these horsemen clearly don't need voice commands—they get more done silently than most of us do with a megaphone.

I think that once you truly strive to understand and communicate with that being known as the horse, voice commands become irrelevant and you head for more "open ground."

*There are those who say that the brain of the horse is no larger than the brain of a turtle, that the horse has no memory and, worse still, no intelligence. Little do such detractors know!*

—from *Sweet William*
by Jessica Palmer

When people find out I have horses, after they ask "don't you have to ride them every day?" their next comment is that they have heard that horses are stupid. Depending on my mood, I either can't bring myself to respond at all or I simply say "Well, I've yet to see a horse light up a cigarette."

We are quick to judge things based on the human idea of intelligence. Yes, horses do things like get tangled in fence wire and cut themselves up badly. But humans put the wire there, expect horses to understand it, and often take no responsibility of thoroughly teaching their horses about yielding to pressure so that perhaps if they get caught in this fence that the human has placed in their life they might stand a chance of knowing that they can yield to the pressure and wait on the human to save them without tearing themselves up in the meantime.

Just because the horse doesn't have the brain power of a human doesn't make it stupid. If we take horses on their own terms, we can get away from this unfair comparison. Horses think like horses. And they think more often than most humans.

*Get mad and chase 'em backward til their tired, then go forward. Been there, done that. Doesn't work, don't bother.*

—Tom McDowell,
professional trainer

Tom McDowell has been a "professional horse trainer" for many years and this kind of frustration is what has led him to search for a better way to educate (i.e., "train") horses. When people like Tom start to change their approach, they are moving toward something that holds more meaning for the horse and not just convenience for the human. What they need for a total breakthrough, in my opinion, is the fundamental change in attitude that they are "educating" horses, not "training" them—and that the horse's owner will need at least as much education, if not more.

*Suppose that whenever [my kids] begin to do something I feel is inappropriate...I yell or intimidate or I threaten or punish and I win. [My] children are outwardly submissive and inwardly rebellious, suppressing feelings that will come out later in uglier ways.*

—from *The 7 Habits of Highly Effective People*
by Stephen Covey

If you take this approach with horses, these large animals will begin to become defensive toward you. The first step to getting beyond this approach is to learn what to do instead of intimidate, threaten, and punish when you are faced with teaching the horse about inappropriate behavior. You might do better concentrating on concepts like "educate," "redirect," or "respect."

*The round pen will give us the ability to gain control
of our horse, without being connected to a thousand-
pound animal that may hurt us.*

—from *Lyons on Horses*
by John Lyons
and Sinclair Browning

Round pens are wonderful—the average one (50'–70' in diameter) is big enough to get some work done but small enough to mentally connect with a loose horse without wearing out the soles of your boots. And they have no corners for the horse to get hung up in. I met a "trainer" once who couldn't understand why anyone would want to be in a round pen with a loose horse who may attack you. I have been fortunate enough to never have had that experience; I would much rather be in a round pen with a loose disrespectful horse than attached to it by a lead rope!

Sometimes, however, round pens have been conveyed as some magic tool. They are simply a tool like anything else and the real benefit of a round pen as a teaching tool is only as effective as the person standing in the middle.

*You can't control a young horse unless you can control yourself.*

—from *The Autobiography of Lincoln Steffens*

All horses will take control of things if you aren't going to, but this is especially true of young horses. They don't have a lot of experience to draw on to tell them that things will most likely work out ok so they have to be more wary. Some are naturally more lenient with the human that others; most will forgive you your mistakes but they won't let you get away with anything!

*Set smaller goals to see greater progress.*

—from the horoscope pages

This quote rang true at a Greg Eliel clinic my mare and I were in. Greg has the ability to take a class of a dozen or more riders and be able to create an environment where each rider feels that the class is individualized for her or him. Greg picked out one "small" thing for me to work on that he knew would have great impact on my overall ride.

Greg saw that I worked too hard to get my mare moving out. He gave me a three-step process to follow every time I wanted my mare to pick up speed, whether it was to actually change gaits or just move out with a little more life in whatever gait she was already in. Greg told me that if I accomplished nothing else, that one thing would be a great advancement for me. By the end of the clinic I only had to get to the second step before she responded and I could begin to feel the next level— only having to do the first step—shaping up.

The small things, if you can find them, can help toward huge progress.

*He flung himself on his horse and rode off madly in all directions.*

—from *Guido the Gimlet of Ghent*
by Stephen Leacock

The image that this quote brings up in my mind makes me chuckle. Sometimes I feel exactly this way!

*If we did all the things we are capable of doing,*
*we would literally astonish ourselves.*

—Thomas Edison,
inventor

Horses are not my profession and therefore my riding tends to go in binges—for a few weeks, I'm riding four or five times a week. Then for a few weeks the rest of my life gets top billing and riding falls by the wayside. On the occasional rides that I fit in during the dry spells I get discouraged because my horse feels like she hasn't progressed much and I feel like I am just a failure at having trained my horse myself. But during the binges, this Edison quote rings true—when I just ride my horse I realize that we have accomplished a lot and are capable of a lot more.

*For every complex problem, there is a solution that is simple, neat, and wrong.*

—H. L. Mencken,
editor

I asked someone whose opinion I respect why she thought that some new equipment seems to solve a particular problem at first, and then the "fix" fades away in a few days, a week, a month. She suggested that perhaps the new equipment was working on new pressure points on the horse that weren't dull yet. The rider who is always looking for these kinds of fixes for the horse instead of working on improving their own feel and timing is constantly (and usually innocently, unwittingly, and with all good intentions) moving on to the next not-yet-dull spot.

*Keep on starting, and finishing will take care of itself.*

—Neil Fiore,
writer

Don't worry about the actual goal—the path to the goal will be more valuable anyway. For instance, one of my ongoing struggles with one of my horses has been to walk through puddles and wet areas without hesitation and without jumping. I have finally started to have increasing success and I don't think it is because we have been exposed to more water spots. I am realizing that I didn't need to spend so much time thinking about my goal—water—but to spend more time working on straightness in my horse. Now if she tries to turn around or skirt the edges of a puddle I can correct, correct, correct her crookedness until she realizes straight ahead is the way to go. Now we need to get to the leaping...

*Do not fear mistakes—there are none.*

—Miles Davis,
musician

$\mathcal{U}$nfortunately with horses there are some things you can do that can turn out to be dangerous—these may be the closest you come to what might be called mistakes. However, if you learn how to be as safe as possible around horses which usually means learning how to teach your horses so that they respect you and act safely around you, you can also become comfortable trying things without fear of making a mistake. If a technique doesn't work, the horse will tell you, you can learn something from it and move on to something that does work.

*An ounce of action is worth a ton of theory.*

—Friedrich Engels,
German socialist

This is an interesting quote to me personally. Over the course of ten-plus years in developing my approach to horses, I came to feel as though I was getting lots closer to understanding good horsemanship intellectually but not a lot closer on a practical level.

Some people can hone their skills on one horse but I knew for me I would learn the most by handling as many different horses as possible, comparing responses and feeling of different horses. But I am not skilled enough to be comfortable working much with other people's horses, even for free. I've been lucky to have a place and been able to afford a small collection of my own, and with each horse I feel a step further along in my ability to act and not just theorize!

*The horse learns from the release, not the pressure.*
*Anyone can pick up on the reins and pull back;*
*it's the timing of the release.*

—Unknown

I was fifteen years old when I first became involved with horses; many of my friends had had horses since they were much younger and had become involved with showing. They would spend hours before a show teaching their horses maneuvers for trail class or positions for showmanship and halter. One thing I didn't understand and didn't ask was "exactly how do you teach a horse something?" It wasn't until I got an unstarted two-year-old and had a huge teaching job ahead of me that was I driven to the point of learning about the concept of the point of release. Ah ha. Here is how you teach a horse something.

---·+·---

*Of course, we could force-break him to everything,*
*but he wouldn't be as good a horse if we did.*
*He'd always be a bit afraid, and he wouldn't mind*
*because he wanted to.*

—from *The Red Pony*
by John Steinbeck

The operative phrase here is "because he wanted to." Even back in 1945 when *The Red Pony* was published, the idea of "making the right thing easy" was alive. There's no question you can get most horses to do what you want them to by intimidating them and making them fearful. But who really wants to have a relationship with a horse that is built on fear? That doesn't feel right to the horse or the human.

*Do the right thing. It will gratify some people,*
*and astonish the rest.*

—Mark Twain,
author

$\mathcal{J}$f you always do the right thing by your horse, you will be amply rewarded. Your horses will definitely show it. The people you really care about will be grateful for your reputation to do the right thing, but mostly you will gratify yourself.

*The longer you ride [a colt] straight, the more braced they become.*

—Buck Brannaman,
horseman

In clinics I have watched and ridden in, Buck Brannaman has often used the game of tag in with the colt-starting group. Once everyone is on their young horses using just a halter and lead rope and milling around together in a controlled area like a round pen, the game starts. Someone is "it" and whoever is "it" has to tag someone else on their left shoulder, and that person becomes "it." No one likes to be in the spotlight so people work pretty hard to avoid being tagged.

Under the supervision of someone as astute a teacher as Buck is, this game accomplishes many things—the riders laugh and relax a little which helps their horses relax; the young horses get accustomed to a lot of other horse/rider combinations milling around and bumping into them; riders learn to how to ask and horses learn to pick up speed in order to avoid being tagged; and the horses get turned a lot.

This turning, done smoothly, really loosens the horse, gets her more flexible and less braced, helps her learn to step under herself, and gives her something to think about besides the new feeling of a rider on her back. The game is fascinating to watch and fun to participate in.

*If you want to have clean ideas, change them as often as you change your shirt.*

—Francis Picabia,
artist

*O*nce I started to grasp this idea of horsemanship that I came across in 1991, I quickly became a committed student. Because of the adamant beliefs I developed in my approach to working with my horses, it can seem that I am not very open-minded when it comes to horses.

Having always considered myself very open-minded, this one-way thinking bothered me. I've decided that I am open to new ideas, but I have developed a strong criteria under which those new ideas must fall. I have developed a baseline against which to judge whether I want to embrace an idea or explore it further. And so I am always looking for new ideas, but many of the ideas I come across aren't very fitting to me because under my criteria they aren't very fitting to the horse. And if that makes me close-minded then I've learned to accept that!

*Let us so live that when we come to die*
*even the undertaker will be sorry.*

—Mark Twain,
author

We can't go through all of life being "perfect"! We all do a little gossiping, we all have had moments when we let impatience take over in our dealings with our horse, we all have committed equine "misdemeanors." But if our intent is always good, and our way of being embraces honesty, then yes, the undertaker and even perhaps a few horses will be sorry when we die. I can't think of a better epitaph to have on my gravestone than "many horses will miss her."

*After about fifteen years or so, you develop your own*
*style and sound and your own boring routines.*

—Janis Ian,
singer

If you had told me over ten years ago that after a decade of studying with some of the best horsemen in the country I would begin to develop my own style, I wouldn't have believed it. Back then, I felt awkward even with a lead rope and my horse walked all over me.

My own style has come about partly as a necessity. I am not a "natural" rider and my hips do not appreciate that I have chosen horseback riding as a hobby. In order for me to get some good riding on my horses, I need to accomplish a lot on the ground. My style is still developing and always will, but in the last year I have come to realize that I do have a "style" and my own methods in my approach to good horsemanship.

*It's easier to fight for one's principles than to live up to them.*

—Alfred Adler,
psychiatrist

Good horsemanship and honest communication with horses results from creating and embracing a set of principles—educate don't train, redirect don't punish, honesty not trickery—and sticking to those principles in all your interactions with your horse. I find it much easier to understand and discuss these principles than to put them into practice, but I'm happy to keep trying.

*You cannot train a horse with shouts and expect it to obey a whisper.*

—from *Letters to My Teacher*
by Dagobert D. Runes

It's sort of like the boy who cried wolf. If you spend most of your time communicating with your horse with harshness and hardness, you will have a long haul ahead of you to get the horse to believe you when you try to communicate from a place of softness and sensitivity. I have talked with a few professional trainers who have changed their methods from "making things happen" to "setting things up and letting them happen." Each of them describe it as a long hard road to not only change their habits but to make their new desired approach such a part of themselves that the horses actually believe it.

*Difficulties mastered are opportunities won.*

—Winston Churchill,
British Prime Minister
in mid-twentieth century

Although sometimes I wish my horse and I would finally get beyond all our difficulties, I do feel a certain amount of pleasure working through an "obstacle." The opportunities that arise at these times include the general one of your horse developing trust in you from getting her through perceived dangers. And each obstacle/difficulty presents specific opportunities such as working on straightness or moving out readily.

A friend once asked my opinion about an issue she was having with one of her horses and she apologetically described her horse as a "work-in-progress." It's not the horse, but the relationship that is a work-in-progress. Those of us who go to clinics regularly do so, I believe, in part because we love the process as much as any end result.

*There is always a slight tendency of the body to sabotage the attention of the mind by providing some distraction.*

—Stephen Spender,
poet

Distractions when it comes to horses can be used to your benefit. If you are working your horse in a round pen in a place where there are absolutely no distractions, what else does your horse have to focus on but you? Bring a dog into the picture (my border collie racing around the outside of the pen comes to mind) or a pen full of pigs nearby or even a day with gusty winds and then see what your horse focuses on. If you can make yourself interesting enough and reliable enough to your horse to get him hooked on you amidst all these distractions, then you know you've succeeded in getting the attention of his mind!

*There are so many stimuli around that sometimes I have
to put myself in a dark room and calm down.*

—Megan Terry

$S$ometimes I feel this way when people are coming at me
with a million different theories about how to interact with
horses. Perhaps I don't go into an actual dark room—more
often than not I go to my computer and crank out a complicated e-mail to my best horse friend and ask her input and
advice on the idea that has been presented to me. After typing
my e-mail (often I don't even have to send it…), I've usually
"calmed down" enough to allow me to see my own principles
clearly and allow them to guide me to conclusions.

*Stop straight. If [your horse] stops crooked, correct it.
If you don't, it will become a lead problem.*

—Buck Brannaman,
horseman

This is great advice in a specific sense, but in general I find it interesting because it shows how the tiniest thing (stopping crooked) may seem unrelated to anything else but in fact can be a real big factor in the successful accomplishment of something big (picking up the correct lead).

*We are tricked by the phenomenon of time—hours and days pass slowly, but years pass quickly.*

—Sally Warner

*S*uddenly as I write this, my "filly" is about to turn seven years old! I got her at six months and up to this point all of her education has been at my hands. I thoroughly enjoy riding her and most times I'm quite proud of what we've accomplished so far, but other times I feel frustrated that she is aging fast and I still feel like there are so many holes in her education that "shouldn't" be there at this point in her life!

*Men make counterfeit money; in many more cases,*
*money makes counterfeit men.*

—Sydney J. Harris

Look for genuineness in the actions and words of the people you learn from. These people know that because they are honest in their dealings with people and with the horse, they don't have chase after money, it will find them.

*It's snowing still. And freezing. However, we haven't had an earthquake lately.*

—Eeyore from *The House on Pooh Corner*
by A.A. Milne

*E*eyore's kind of optimism would help all of us horse people! We get so hung up on the things that have gone wrong that we forget to take pleasure in the things that are going right.

*I hope that I may always desire more than
I can accomplish.*

—Michaelangelo,
artist

My little mare has some bratty aspects to her attitude and a respected clinician advised me that I could, now that she was a little older, firm up on her a little more. So I did, and it was an important thing to do at that stage, but then I found her responding as if anticipating my firmness. Lately I've been trying to work my way back to a place somewhere in between. Whether I can accomplish that or not, it is what I desire and I'm sure that when/if I do accomplish it we'll have come up with other things to desire.

*Procrastination means you know what you need to do
and you don't do it. If you don't know what to do,
you aren't procrastinating. You are thinking.*

—from *The Procrastinator's Guide to Success*
by Lynn Lively

I don't know about you, but I do a lot of thinking!

My horses are on my mind most of the time—while driving, while doing barn chores, while showering, I'm sure even while sleeping. I think a lot about the last ride and what went smoothly, and where there were some rough places. My mare and border collie and I often take short evening rides through the trails on our property. It took me months to be able to do this because my mare was pretty hooked on her pals back at the barn. With each ride, we got farther before the sticky moment showed up. Now there are two or three remaining spots that are always on my mind between rides—where does she start to balk, how can I get to her earlier so she doesn't get all the way to actually stopping and fussing, should I trot or walk toward those spots? Maybe if I would stop thinking about those spots they would simply go away!

*The trouble with our conscious mind is that it tries too hard.*

—R. Reid Wilson

I find that if I have an audience of more than one or two people while working with a horse, I become too conscious of my actions. My interactions with the horse become stiff and unnatural. It's a little better when I'm working with one of my own horses than the rare occasions that I am handling or riding someone else's horse. But over the years as my abilities have developed and I have enough of my own approach, this has gotten better. I've become a little less "conscious" and a little more natural. It all takes a while.

*Truth is a hard master, and costly to serve, but it simplifies all problems.*

—from *Brother Cadfael's Penance*
by Ellis Peters

If you always harken back to the truth—true feelings, true actions, true beliefs—you will have a permanent parameter within which you interact with everything in life, including horses.

*It's better to give children rules to break than to give them no rules at all.*

—Tipper Gore,
former Second Lady

Another concept that applies to horses as well as children. Although the word "rules" holds a bit of a domineering connotation—humans hold the rules and horses must follow them—if we want to be safe around out horses we simply do need to set parameters. But then we hold the responsibility of helping our horses understand those rules. One way is to give them the opportunity to break a rule. Then they are able to compare what it is you want and what you don't want. And finally, when they do break the rules, we the rule-setters need to avoid anger and punishment but rather simply use the opportunity to explain (or re-explain!) the rules.

*Those who know others are intelligent.*
*Those who know themselves have insight.*

—Lao-tzu,
Chinese philosopher

There are not too many things we can do in the world that will give us such an immediate and often graphic response to our actions as interacting with a horse will. In this way, horses can help us know ourselves—how do we act and how do our actions affect other beings?

*A real horseman must also be able to ... realize that a
horse is not equipped with* human *understanding.*

—from *Horsemanship*
by Waldemar Seunig

This is one of the more frustrating and contentious elements
of interacting with horses. And perhaps one of the most miscon-
strued thoughts about what so-called "natural horsemanship" is
all about.

Much of the way we expect horses to react and behave
revolves around this ability for human understanding. I think
that we gain much more out of our relationship with horses and
we can take that relationship and communication with horses to
a much higher level if we accept the fact that they do not have
the same thought-processing ability as we do.

However, I also don't feel that acceptance of this fact needs
to lead us to "acting like a horse" or creating a new "language" in
order to communicate with horses. For instance, we don't need
to run around using a tree branch to pretend we have a tail—
that, in my opinion, is demeaning to the horse (not to mention
the human).

Ultimately, the horse and human can both be what they are
and still have a phenomenal relationship and a high level of
communication.

———·•·———

*There are really no mistakes in life—only lessons.*

—Anonymous

Well, we've all heard this one before but sometimes it sure can seem like things are a mistake—especially if the lesson comes way later! Horses can be so dangerous that we certainly don't want our mistakes to become *someone else's* lesson. But it is a real reminder to get to the point of being able not only to accept mistakes but not be afraid to make them.

I jokingly refer to my first horse as "mistake number one" and my second as "mistake number two" and so on. My mare definitely benefited from my "mistakes" with my gelding. I'm hoping my filly will be able to preserve a lot more of her sensitivity because of my mistakes—i.e., lessons—with the first two.

*You have freedom when you're easy in your harness.*

—Robert Frost,
poet

We are all confined in some way or another—a job, a routine, a house, even our clothes are a certain amount of confinement. In order for us to have horses, they too have many levels of confinement—a stall, a paddock, a bridle, a halter. Even in a 300-acre pasture horses will eventually come to fences!

However, if a horse is "easy in its harness," if you pay attention to the horse's mental soundness, the horse can be free within that confinement. When a horse feels mentally free, he seems not nearly as concerned with the physical. I believe the mentally free horse even enjoys lounging in box stall once in a while if he's not confined to it 21 hours a day.

*Mona: I had trouble with my horse yesterday. I wanted to go in one direction and he wanted to go in another.*

*Sam: So how did you decide?*

*Mona: He tossed me for it.*

—from *The Everything Kids' Joke Book*
by Michael Dahl

I've been tossed a few times for wanting to go in a different direction from my horse, so this joke left me chuckling. Of course, since then I've tried to learn as much as possible about making my idea my horse's idea so we don't run up against as many times when he thinks he has to "toss" me for it.

*As far as I'm concerned, a rider's fear is real—it's a nonnegotiable issue. What feels like to her is what it is. Period. It doesn't matter whether her trainer, buddy, college professor, mother, or grandfather thinks she is overreacting, overprotective, or overindulgent.*

—from *Heads Up!*
by Janet Sasson Edgette, Psy.D.

No one has the right to tell you how you feel about any-thing—they are your feelings and that's that! However, that doesn't mean you can't learn to feel differently about something. With horses, that typically means overcoming fear.

I have always been a somewhat fearful rider, especially of speed. Since I am not what is often referred to as a "natural" rider, I have to spend a lot of time concentrating and readjust-ing. Put some speed on it, and my seat falls apart pretty quickly!

The one thing that has taken away a lot of my fear is having learned the importance of being able to direct my horse's feet—with my young horses, this is what I concentrate on teaching them first, and what I've focused a lot on learning myself.

*Do not wish to be anything but what you are, and try to be that perfectly.*

—St Francis de Sales

Trying to do things perfectly is probably the best way to go about everything. That said, you can also really stifle your ability to make any progress by always expecting perfection from yourself. Horses seem to react negatively to being picked on or drilled in the name of perfection. I think it helps to try to be perfect in small steps. Instead of getting a whole maneuver perfect in one or two sessions, work on one step of the maneuver at a time so you both can feel successful and when you are both ready, put all the perfect steps together!

*Those who claim it is "unethical" to ask a horse to do anything it would not do of its own inclination are being naïve and foolish; but equally naïve and foolish are those who expect to teach a horse to do their bidding without taking into consideration its natural inclinations.*

—from *The Nature of Horses*
by Stephen Budiansky

Many people get annoyed if they are working their horse in an arena and she keeps heading toward the gate. In fact, it can build into something that can take a lot of "unbuilding."

However, you can also use that tendency to want to head to the gate to teach the horse some things. One of the clinicians I've ridden with made the point that perhaps you could use the gate on something that requires forward movement. Use the gate to pick up a faster gait or move right out from a standstill. Or put an obstacle in the way—a caveletti or a big tarp—and use the gate to help teach your horse about being forward and straight right over the obstacle.

In the meantime, you are making things more clear and interesting to the horse, which just might be what it takes to get the horse to take more of an interest in working with you than wanting out the gate. It's all in the attitude you take to things.

*If they feel like they can't move, that's all they think
about. If they feel like they can move, they usually don't.*

—Joe Wolter from "Another Approach"
in *America's Horse*

The self-preservation instinct in the horse makes the ability to move of supreme importance to the horse. Being always mindful of the level of importance this holds to the horse helps people better get along with the horse.

People seem to spend most of their time trying to confine the horse with things like crossties, nose chains, and other physical restraints. I've watched people using a flag on a horse or other things to sack it out with and while they are presenting it to the horse they are holding onto the horse tightly at the chin. Giving the horse more freedom offers her the trust that if the ability to move is there she won't use it unless she absolutely has to. And when she absolutely has to, the fact that she can, along with your support, will help her to stop sooner and face or accept or investigate whatever it is that is making her feel the need to move.

*...the wise horseman has accepted the horse on his own terms and enhanced both their spirits by what they have learned together.*

—from *Beyond the Mirrors*
by Jill Keisler Hassler

While accepting the horse on his own terms is perhaps the main turning point in having a better relationship with our horse, it doesn't mean letting a horse walk all over you either. A common misperception I've heard about so-called "natural horsemanship" is that it is a soft-touch approach and that the term "natural" means letting the horse do what comes natural to it no matter what. But natural horsemanship simply means, to me, understanding how to use your horse's natural instincts to the advantage of both of you in developing a strong relationship, including one of respect. And respect to the horse, in my mind, doesn't mean treating a horse like a puppy; and respect to the human doesn't include being stepped on or knocked around or nibbled at by a 1,000-pound animal.

So accepting the horse on its own terms has to also include those terms being within the boundaries of safety for humans and horses interacting.

*Is there a split between mind and body, and if so, which is better to have?*

—Woody Allen
in *Getting Even*

This topic has been of ongoing interest to me. Which is more beneficial, a sound mind or a sound body? Clearly with horses there are certain physical unsoundnesses that make the horse impossible to ride. But beyond that, which is best to put first?

Ultimately, with the help of many discussions with friends and many questions to clinicians, I have decided this about the physical versus mental thing: all horses, like people, have different tolerance levels for discomfort and that for the most part horses who have a sound mind can better withstand some physical discomfort. That's certainly not to say that we shouldn't do what we can to make our horses physically comfortable—proper and regular farrier attention, veterinary maintenance, the very best tack you can afford. But I think a lot of people focus excessively on the physical because it is more visible; if they spend some concerted effort to learn to "see" the mental horse, they would redirect some of that focus and some of the physical would take care of itself.

*The only thing I can change is myself, but sometimes that makes all the difference.*

—Anonymous

Since I am short, I have gotten pretty good at teaching my horses to come up to the fence so I can get on without looking like (and feeling like) I'm scaling a cliff. My seven-year-old mare positions herself perfectly, right down to the last footstep.

When the time came to take my first ride on my younger filly at a clinic, I worked at getting her up to the fence. We had worked on this a lot over the past few months and she would get pretty close but not as close as I felt she could based on our work we'd done. Finally, after a few times of failing to get her to take that last perfect step and having to start over, the clinician suggested that he would have simply moved himself down fence a step or two to line up with her, and got on.

Hmm, there was a thought. All these new experiences and activity going on around us probably made coming up to the fence a bit different experience from the past.

Of course, there comes a time in the horse's education when you can get particular about a thing like that. But in this case, this was not the right time to get so picky about it. I was too focused on getting her to adjust to me. While I felt badly and a bit discouraged with myself, ultimately, the incident allowed me to (once again) learn a good lesson—the horse doesn't have to do all the adjusting! I could do one small thing myself to make it work out.

*When a man is once well run away with, the first thing that occurs to him, I imagine, is how to stop his horse; but men by no means agree in the modes of bringing this matter about.*

—from *An Academy for Grown Horsemen*
by Geoffrey Gambardo

Most of the clinics I have attended in the past decade have emphasized teaching your horse something referred to as "the one-rein stop" as a safety device to disengage the horse's hindquarters and stop a runaway situation. The one-rein stop has not only helped me out of potentially bad situations like uncontrolled galloping and even bucking, but it also has made me a more confident rider—that I have this tool to call upon so I don't need to be fearful of what might come up. It can sometimes be tough to perform if you are on a tight trail or you might not want to pull a horse's head way around while they are at a full gallop. If you work on the one-rein stop enough you don't have to pull the head completely around but can pick up just enough on one rein to start to break the impulsion enough to regain control.

*There are no secrets to success. It is the result of preparation, hard work, and learning from failure.*

—Colin L. Powell,
Secretary of State

There was a time when I couldn't imagine why anyone wouldn't want to learn the approach to horsemanship that I have become exposed to in clinics over the past decade. I started thinking about how I've attended dozens of clinics in those ten years. The logistics of getting there is hard work not to mention the fact that you ride in all kinds of exhausting weather, concentrate on learning all day for days in a row, try new things with your horse, and have all sorts of work to do ahead of time to clear your schedule and catch up after the clinic is over. This approach is extremely hard work and I've come to the conclusion that there are simply a lot of people for whom it is just too much of a commitment.

I certainly don't want to give the impression that those of us who are willing to learn it are more right than those who are not. But many clinicians say in every class they have people who come to them as a final resort—things are really not working out for them. Up to that point, the horse did a lot of filling in, they were lucky, or whatever.

I'd rather be more proactive and go learn good horsemanship whether I need it or not, than be reactive and learn good horsemanship because something bad happened.

*Mindful awareness of different options gives us greater control. The feeling of greater control, in turn, encourages us to be more mindful. Rather than being a chore, mindfulness engages us in a continuing momentum.*

—from *Mindfulness*
by Ellen Langer

$O$nce I became extremely engaged by what I was learning about working with horses (which was about five minutes into my first Buck Brannaman clinic), none of the effort I've put in for the subsequent years has seemed like a chore at all. Don't get me wrong, it was hard work, frustrating, and exasperating along with all the good stuff, but the more I worked at it, the easier my horses became to be around. The easier my horses became to be around, the more I wanted to be around them. The more I wanted to be around them, the better I wanted my interactions with them to be.

*Don't concentrate so much on life's big joys that you miss the small ones.*

—Anonymous

J can get so focused in my horsemanship on something huge that I forget to recognize our smaller accomplishments. Being able to just load up your horse and join a bunch of friends on a trail ride is a big accomplishment in a young horse's education. But there are smaller, day-to-day things that are just as great, like a horse who respects your space, a horse that stands still when you mount up, a horse who can step its hindquarters over to get you out of the gate without the rest of the herd following. Those things are worth noticing!

*You can never learn less, you can only learn more.*

—R. Buckminster Fuller,
engineer

Although sometimes when my horse and I are in one of our "regression" periods and I feel like we are "learning less," it is reassuring to know that once you've learned something you have learned it, and there's only more to learn. Even when you don't feel like you've got something down, you've learned it even if only enough to know you aren't doing it!

*The horse has an immense capacity to learn, but it is
the way in which he has already been taught that is
revealed in his behaviour.*

—from *Equus Caballus*
by Jan May

 $M$ any people think that if you can get a halter on a horse
and get it from one place to another, then it is halter broke. The
horse's behavior on the end of the halter determines whether or
not it is halter broke, not the fact that it has a halter on its head.
Clinicians can tell just by watching a horse being led and by
working with it in the round pen if the horse has been hand fed,
lunged, trained on with side reins, etc. The horse tells us these
things about how he has been taught by his behavior in any
given situation, especially ones where it is a little stressful for
him like a clinic where he is being asked to do things he has
never really been asked to do before (like not walk all over the
person leading him).

*The greatest power is often simple patience.*

—E. Joseph Cossman,
entrepreneur

Patience is clearly a key to being successful with teaching horses. And the less skilled you are with feel and timing, the more patient you need to be while your horse figures out what it is you are asking of her. The horse didn't request that it come live with you and please, please lock me in a stall or corral and ride and feed me according to your convenience. So I believe the onus is on us to muster up the patience to teach the horse what we have determined we need it to know to live comfortably under our parameters.

*"Tricks" have no place in the art of riding, since in moments of crisis, when effective action is most needed, the superficial "trick" never succeeds.*

—from *Give Your Horse a Chance*
by Lt. Col. A. L. D'Endrody

What is considered to be a "trick" is a variable thing! I tend to feel this statement applies to "clickers" and that if push really came to shove (which is different for all horses!), the clicker would mean nothing to the horse as an effective action in a moment of real crisis. That said, I have friends who have very successful relationships with their horses based on clicker train-ing; and certainly there are many convincing books written about it and training programs based on it!

However, if something appears to me to be superficial and has nothing to do with feel, I am not interested in it. I want to ride my horse in any circumstance and feel like it takes nothing more than hers and my relationship to deal with a situation. I am not there yet, and may never be, but that's my goal.

*It doesn't matter what [style of gear] you have on your horse, it's how he understands what you are trying to do.*

—Ray Hunt
at a clinic

A question I get asked when people learn I have horses is if I ride English or Western. I have come to simply say "both." I really make no distinction in how I ride and I find it odd that people would. It would be like driving differently when you get in a different car—sure, the dials may be in a different place and you may have to accommodate for a longer wheel base or whatever, but basically, driving is driving. You go by stepping on the gas, stop by stepping on the brake, turn the steering wheel to turn the vehicle.

When I am in the saddle, I want the same things—a soft feel when I pick up the reins, my horse to step away from my leg pressure—no matter what type of saddle I'm sitting in.

*To learn, you have to listen, to improve you have to try.*

—Unknown

$\int$ used to be worried I was going to try something with my horse, do it wrong, and "ruin" her. After dozens of clinics, it finally sunk in that even the best horsemen and horsewomen in the world had a period of learning and experimenting where what they were trying to do didn't shape up as fast or as well as it does now. And most of my teachers have learned by working with thousands of horses—I've only had five horses under my sole care in my life (so far…) and handled maybe two dozen others, so I guess I can cut myself a break!

*If your success is not on your own terms, if it looks good
to the world but does not feel good in your heart,
it is not success at all.*

—Anna Quindlen, writer

When I bought my second horse—13 years after I'd sold my first one—I was frustrated by my lack of skill in handling this strong two-year-old gelding. Once that summer when his feet were being trimmed, he didn't behave quite to the liking of the farrier, who reacted by thrashing the horse around the aisle of the barn. Things were flying off the walls. After this little session, my horse nearly saluted the farrier. The farrier explained to me that I was too timid with the horse and needed to learn how to do what he just did.

I was impressed by the results and appalled by the method. I didn't need or want my horse to salute me, but I sure would appreciate the focus and attention! Although the appearance of "success" was right in front of my eyes, I sure wasn't feeling in my heart that it was a good way to get there, or that I was even witnessing success. I decided from that moment on that—although I couldn't explain it at the time—I wanted to find a way to have an attentive, focused horse that came from respect and trust of me, not from fear of me. If I couldn't find it, then that was it for me and horses.

I feel eternally grateful to have found "it," even though I am a long way from perfecting the method. But any success I have with my horses is definitely heartfelt from the sincere desire for mutual respect.

*The way to the goal is not to be measured! Of what importance are weeks, months, years?*

—from *Zen in the Art of Archery*
by Eugen Herrigel

It took me a while, but I finally have stopped worrying about how long it takes for me to accomplish some phase of my horses' education. I have absolutely no time issues when it comes to horses—they are not a means to an end for me, they are an end in themselves. If I start a youngster and it is four years before I can lope her on a trail with a loose rein, so be it. It won't be for lack of trying, but I certainly feel no compulsion to rush either myself or the horse beyond our capability at any given point. If I were riding competitively, I would feel a little differently, but I actually think that more the opposite, it is that lack of wanting to rush the horse (and myself) to meet some artificial goal that is the very reason why I have little interest in riding in competition.

*There is many a "rider" in full paraphernalia who has
his horses trained by somebody else, who mounts them
for horse shows only, who has never trained a horse
himself, and who therefore will never understand
that it is he himself who has to learn from the horse
if he strives to reach the highest level of equitation.*

—from *My Horses, My Teachers*
by Alois Podhajsky

When I chatted with the sponsor before the first "natural horsemanship" clinic I attended, I asked her about sending my gelding off to a trainer after the clinic. Her response was "why would you want to do that?" I just thought that was what one did with a young horse. I did end up sending him for two months to a "trainer" simply to get him some riding experience after my novice ability wound up with me on the ground a few too many times. But after a few years and two more youngsters I began to see the reason for her question. I may still some day want to have someone else ride a horse for me a few times, but the idea of shipping a horse off to a "professional trainer" doesn't even cross my mind. For both of us to spend some time with a coach or teacher makes sense; it is extremely important to me to learn how to educate my horses myself.

*That which grows fast, withers rapidly. That which grows slowly, endures.*

—Josiah Gilbert Holland

Many times I have heard clinicians say that sometimes the slowest route is the fastest way to get where you want to go. Horses are often, because of human time constraints, forced to do things at ages that they are barely physically able to do what is being asked. Those of us who are no more than pleasure riders can learn to educate our horses at whatever speed works for the horse and have what we teach them last rather than have something hold together only long enough to get through a ten-minute class at a horse show.

*No time spent in the saddle is wasted; as you learn to communicate with the horse and appreciate what he can do for you, it will add a fascinating dimension to your life.*

—from *The Handbook of Riding*
by Mary Gordon-Watson

I had a horse for two years when I was around 20, and then left horses for over a decade before getting back into them again. I currently have four horses of my own and I can't imagine not being able to interact with a horse every day. But my experience with horses now is so completely different from back when I was twenty that I can't even describe it to my friends who knew me when I had that filly so many years ago. I know it is this whole idea of learning to communicate with my horses that has added a "fascinating dimension" to my life.

*You will only be remembered for two things:*
*the problems you solve and the ones you create.*

—from *101 Wisdom Keys*
by Mike Murdock

I don't know if I believe this quote to be true—I remember people for lots of things that have nothing to do with problems. But what it says to me is that creating and solving problems is a huge thing in our lives. And it certainly is in our horse life.

Whenever I come upon a "problem" with one of my horses, it reminds me of my continued quest to be mindful of those little things that can lead up to what we consider to be problems. Of course, my horses don't think about problems, they just live their lives!

*It's a rule of nature that taking a day off on a farm
sets a person back at least a week.*

—from *A Map of the World*
by Jane Hamilton

One great thing about working with horses is that "taking a day off" doesn't have to set you back at all. (Taking a day off from barn chores, however, is a different story!) I believe horses don't know the time between "sessions." If you interact with your horses with quality and consistency every time, and your riding and handling sessions end on the most positive note possible, and they just remember the last time they interacted with you and associate it with a positive experience or a negative experience.

*How many a man has thrown up his hands at a time
when a little more effort, a little more patience would
have achieved success?*

—Elbert Hubbard,
editor

You'll never know if you gave up right before things were
going to work out, so why give up? If what you had in mind to
accomplish with your horse has come down to a battle, perhaps
you might postpone trying to reach that ultimate goal—a flying
lead change, for instance—and work on one of the earlier steps
to that goal—shifting the horse's shoulders over—but that isn't
giving up on the goal, it's building on the steps to that goal.

APRIL 27

---

*When eating fruit, think of the person who planted
the tree.*

—Vietnamese proverb

There is always someone to be thankful for. I feel lucky to
have run across some great equine mentors just at the moment
when I needed them the most. My horse life changed dramati-
cally because of it, and every time I have a moment of unity
with one of my horses, I definitely think of those mentors.

*Experience is that marvelous thing that enables you to recognize a mistake when you make it again.*

—F. P. Jones

While we would like to have our experience enable us not to make the same mistake twice, I have begun to feel fortunate to even recognize the same mistake. Preventing it from happening again may come with twenty or thirty years more experience. But by then I'll have made loads of new mistakes to keep track of!

*If you do the little jobs well, the big ones tend to take care of themselves.*

—Dale Carnegie

In my own horsemanship, this reminds me of shoeing time with my mare. She tends to be impatient in general, and with slightly complicated shoeing needs, it takes a good amount of time to shoe her and really tests her patience.

Most people who have given me advice have tended toward what to do with her during the actual shoeing—herbal remedies, acupressure points, etc. I do try to help her relax and I try to work her in the round pen before the farrier comes to give her a chance to move her feet some before she has to stand still for so long (and to get some focus). But the real key to continued improvement has been to work on the advice my farrier has given me.

He focuses on little things that may seem unrelated to shoeing, but actually help her help him get things done more efficiently—like working on yielding so I can ask her to rock her weight back or forward without moving a foot, or learning more about directing her feet so I can move one foot and not her whole body or teaching her to understand that when the lead rope is slack in my hand, she shouldn't move her feet. Once these little things are firmly in place, they add up to the big thing like an easier shoeing job.

*Natural talent, no matter how great, can't make up for a lack of basic knowledge and skills—but solid basics, combined with real desire and commitment, can make any rider a good rider.*

—from *Anne Kursinski's Riding and Jumping Clinic* by Anne Kursinski with Miranda Lorraine

Having little "natural" talent when it comes to horses, this quote made me feel much better! I can learn, even if it's slowly, and I have the desire and certainly the commitment to work toward "true unity" with horses so I feel I've been able to become a better rider with aspirations to someday be a "good rider."

*Before everything else, getting ready is the secret of success.*

—Henry Ford,
auto manufacturer

In all of the clinics I have attended, I have heard over and over again about the importance of preparing your horse for a transition. This is important whether it's for something as dramatic as a change from one gait to another, or as simple as picking up a foot to clean a hoof.

For instance, in picking up a foot, we need to be aware if the horse is bearing weight on that foot and allow him the chance to prepare himself to have that foot picked up. When asking for a new gait or a lead change, being aware of what position the horse is in and waiting until he is in proper position to accomplish what we are asking allows both horse and rider to be successful. I find this difficult but the more small instances in which I feel this, the more in tune with my horse that I feel. We need to be the partner our horse needs in order to have them be the partner we want them to be. We can do that through awareness.

*Never give up and never give in.*

—Hubert H. Humphrey,
politician

I believe that in order to work toward unity with my horses I may need to make some concessions in the short-term in order to have long-term success. My mare and her barn sourness is a good example. At a certain fork in the trail in the woods behind my house, she would stop and be quite adamant about wanting to go right back to the barn. This became quite an argument between us. Finally, I stopped going to that point for a while, and just rode where she was comfortable going, avoiding the arguments all together. My intention was to get her more comfortable with just going for a ride away from the barn and that our rides would not end up in arguments. The last time I rode her through the woods, she did not balk at all at the crossroad. Approaching it like this may be a sort of "giving in" but ultimately by making those small concessions you are not giving up on your greater goal of good horsemanship.

*Shoot for the moon. Even if you miss, you'll land among the stars.*

—Anonymous

Quite often I say to myself "If Ray Hunt were handling this horse..." or "Buck Brannaman would accomplish in one afternoon what it takes me three years to get done." This is usually followed by "since I'm not Ray Hunt or Buck Brannaman..." But even though I will never be as good as these men or any other of the horsemen and horsewomen that I admire and try to learn from, I still have the desire to be as good as I possibly can be in my interactions with horses. So if I shoot to be as good as these world-class horsemen, maybe I'll at least some day land among my peers.

———·•·———

*Remember, a horse is a horse.*

—from *Horse, Follow Closely*
by GaWaNi Pony Boy

$\mathcal{I}$n his book, *Horse, Follow Closely*, GaWaNi Pony Boy speaks of "creating the right environment…in which two beings can understand each other." I like this idea, it seems to get pretty close to the elusive description of the "true unity." The horse is completely at the mercy of the environment that we provide. At the least, we can meet him partway with an environment conducive to the horse's natural way of being. With this environment comes a comfort level for the horse that allows us to begin to understand each other.

*Mr. Luard's impressions, mainly of the horse working in streets or fields rather than the pampered animal in the paddock, are vivid...he combines the perception of movement with high skill and judgment.*

—from *Horses and Movement:*
*Drawings and Paintings by Lowes Dalbiac Luard,*
Edited by Oliver Beckett

This is a fabulous book—it may now be out of print but I found a copy browsing in the remainder section of a huge book outlet called The New England Mobile Book Fair in Newton Heights, Massachusetts. It includes paintings and sketches of horses and mules pulling heavy loads. The head and neck positions that the horse takes on to do these jobs is almost painful to look at—and it made me realize how seldom we actually see horses work hard these days. With the horse's lack of "real work" in our society, we are now more comfortable with the poses of our real horses that resemble those plastic horse statues than horses working.

*In matters of style, swim with the current; in matters of principle, stand like a rock.*

—Thomas Jefferson,
3rd U.S. President

If I am going to perform in a stadium jumping class, clearly I need to ride in an English hunter-jumper saddle, wear breeches, don the expected coat, get into position over jumps, etc. This is style.

But I am determined to adhere to the principles of good horsemanship that I have strived to learn over the past decade. So if I would compete, I would not hold the reins so tight that if someone cut them I'd shoot off the back like a rocket. I would not use a martingale to keep my horse's head down, I would have taught my horse to yield when I picked up contact on the reins. I would not put a fly bonnet on my horse to muffle the crowd sounds, I would have properly accustomed my horse to the crowds she would be expected to perform with even if it meant not winning a few times to get to that point. Easy to say by an armchair hunter-jumper, I know, but I expect top-level horsemanship from these people with top-level equitation. Following style is easy, upholding your principles is difficult.

*A conditioned way of perceiving the world categorizes situations simplistically and evokes habitual responses, both inwardly and outwardly.*

—from *Living the Mindful Life*
by Charles T. Tart

Conditioned-response training is popular and certainly works. In fact, I think it is probably difficult not to incorporate some conditioned response in the education of the animals we interact with daily, no matter what your overall approach is. My horses know that when they see me coming carrying little white buckets, it's feeding time and they all head to their respective feed tubs.

Although I haven't done a scientific study, I have personally observed that horses (and dogs) who have been subjects of conditioned-response training have a faraway look in their eyes when they are interacting with humans.

I have also observed many times that when these same horses come to a clinic where their owners begin to learn how to interact with them with feel and ways that hold meaning to the horse, the horse's eyes brighten, their whole way of being changes, they lose that bored look, and they become intrigued and interested in the world around them.

*Small opportunities are often the beginning of great enterprises.*

—Demosthenes,
Greek orator

I occasionally take my mare to a local show ring in the middle of the week just to mess around somewhere different. One day there was, she soon informed me, a horse-eating barrel on one side of the ring. The first time around she got that highly animated look and was turning at it and snorting and prancing and wanting to bolt. This small opportunity turned into a "great enterprise" of learning. I could use some of the advice I'd learned from a couple clinics to use this as an opportunity to let my mare gain another step in her trust of me.

We rode around the ring both ways numerous times and every time we got near the barrel, I would reassure her with pats and words, and ride her as close to the barrel as she dared, maybe just a tad closer, but still a pretty wide swing at first. Sometimes I would change direction right before the barrel, which seemed to make her not only less afraid of it, but also more curious about it. By the time we were ready to leave, she was completely unimpressed with the barrel, rode around the ring right on the rail, and walked right over to the barrel when I offered her the opportunity to check it out.

*Even when he has become skilled in [the use of this method], he will find that each horse he handles will always require study and thought.*

—from *Reinsman of the West: Bits and Bridles*
by Ed Connell

Although I have only "started" three young horses since my re-entry to the horse world a decade ago, each of these three have been quite different from each other, and "study and thought" have ruled my world with them. The first, a Quarter Horse gelding, Bud, has been in my mind almost constantly for the decade-plus since I got him. I will probably be a student of Bud's for all his days and more. He doesn't much like being patted and I am always searching for that right spot where I can offer him some affection. He has been difficult to ride and I have "re-started" him several times. Bud is constantly on my mind.

*It's up to us to explain [to young horses] what we expect when we're near. If we don't, they'll simply never know.*

—from *Considering the Horse*
by Mark Rashid

I agree with Mark Rashid's quote with all my heart. If we do not want our horses to push on us, drag us around, step on our feet, snack on the trail, whatever it is, we need to teach them what we do expect, that's only fair.

For example, I work hard to teach my horses that when I come into their turnout with an armful of hay, I am not to be accosted! Although my mare bosses my filly around when they are out together, when I am leading that filly through the pasture or corral she is in my hands and, my mare has had to learn, completely off limits to my mare—but my mare didn't know that until I told her that even with this horse who is lower on the pecking order attached to me, I am still the leader.

*I knew that I should never write as well as I could wish,
but I thought, with pains, that I could arrive at writing
as well as my natural defects allowed.*

—W. Somerset Maugham,
author

Maughams's writing talent was sufficient enough for him to
become a well-known writer. And while I daresay the great
majority of us who have horses don't have any aspirations to
become well known for our equestrian talents, I think this quote
points out rather neatly that we might best be pleased with the
level of talent we do have!

*Resistance causes pain and lethargy. It is when we practice acceptance that new possibilities appear.*

—Anonymous

From what I have seen over the past decade of studying good horsemanship, developing a yielding frame of mind in a horse is perhaps the most noble and most important thing of all. A horse who yields rather than resists is the safest and most content horse to be around. And when they are in a yielding frame of mind their mental energy is free for learning and cooperation instead of being used up resisting and building braces that ultimately often become part of the cycle of physical unsoundness.

*The first thing we have to do in our practice is to reveal things as they are.*

—Thich Nhat Hanh,
Buddhist monk

Many times when a particularly troubled horse is worked with in a clinic, the owner often makes a lot of excuses for his behavior. The horse, ever living in the present, simply tells it like it is. He doesn't try to hide his behavior and he certainly doesn't make excuses for it. It no longer matters so much the history of the horse's negative behavior—once you've made that important decision to help the horse and give him a reason to change his outlook on life then it's fine to simply let things reveal themselves so they can be taken head on and dealt with.

*Ride the horse in the direction that it's going.*

—Werner Erhard

$S$ometimes the best thing to do is to go with the flow. This quote once more reminds me of a way to approach herd-boundness. By starting to work through this by simply riding the horse in the direction she goes instead of trying to force her to go in directions she doesn't want to go, you can get forwardness and eliminate the arguments. Then you can begin to expand the horse's comfort range and offer direction. Eliminating the arguments can get rid of some of the negative energy from both of you.

*One never notices what has been done; one can only see what remains to be done....*

—Marie Curie,
chemist

My Quarter Horse mare is currently my "best riding horse." I can list a couple pages of things we have accomplished together since I got her as a yearling—she loads readily into a trailer, she stands without being tied for brushing and saddling, I can stand on my picnic table and move her feet to the exact position I want them in to mount, and many other things that make our life together rewarding and peaceful.

But I am usually more inclined to recite what we can't yet do—canter in small circles, flying lead changes, or even ride away from our barn and her two pasture mates without some barn/herd sour episode somewhere at one of the forks in our trails.

It took starting my young Arab to really be able to appreciate all that my older mare and I have, in fact, accomplished!

*The world is quickly bored by the recital of misfortune...*

—W. Somerset Maugham,
author

We all have struggles with our horsemanship, and therefore our horses, probably almost daily. But our circle of friends, no matter how close and no matter how much support we provide each other, become weary of neverending discussions of problems, just as we become weary of hearing them from others.

My now teenaged gelding has been a source of fascination for me since I got him 11 years ago—the fascination has mostly not been of the "good" kind. And I have talked about him a lot. When he was the focus of my horse life, before I got my mare and my newest filly, my friends surely got tired of hearing all my tales of woe about Bud. I know this because even I got sick of talking about him!

Maybe a side benefit to realizing that you are probably boring your friends with your constant recital of misfortune is that it can help to start looking at the more positive stuff going on with your horse—and then you can build on those things rather than keeping the focus on the negative things.

---

*Advice is what we ask for when we already know the answer but wish we didn't.*

—Erica Jong,
author

I call this the "confirmation factor." I've been in the book publishing field a long time and I've seen a lot of manuscripts and even bestselling books that make me think "why is a book with such an obvious message so popular?" Sometimes we just need confirmation from others—usually from people whose opinion we respect—that we have been doing the right thing.

But sometimes, as Jong points out, we seek the confirmation of something that we wish wasn't the case—maybe it's time to move on to a horse more fitting of our skill level, maybe it's time to get help, maybe it's best to stay in the round pen and get out on the trails next year. It helps when someone else confirms your instinct.

*It's ok if you mess up. You should give yourself a break.*

—Billy Joel,
musician

If you are mindful of what happened, "messing up" can often provide opportunities for learning for both you and your horse. Even the most experienced horsemen and horsewomen mess up once in a while—it is their years of experience that helps them see the lesson in their mistake.

*As soon as you trust yourself you will know how to live.*

—Johann von Goethe,
poet

If you can't trust yourself, who can you trust? And you have complete control over whether or not to trust yourself, so why not start right now? I have come to trust my ability to recognize things that fit into my fundamental way of being, including my approach to horsemanship. This allows me to walk into a horse clinic and know almost the minute the clinician opens her or his mouth (actually, usually before…) whether or not this is someone I am interested in learning from.

*You have to be brave to make mistakes in public.*

—Louise Page

The best horsemen who are offering clinics are the ones who don't need to prescreen the horses they will work with or do rehearsals. They're confident enough of their knowledge to risk making mistakes in front of their audience. The clinicians who are more "showmen" than "horsemen" are more concerned about how they will look to an audience and therefore are careful to pick horses that will make them look successful. Although there is still plenty to learn from them, I stay away from the latter kind of clinicians; I am more interested in what the clinician does for the horse, not a demonstration of how good the clinician makes himself or herself seem.

*Those who discuss [happiness] lack it.*

—Holbrook Johnson

Discussing happiness is sort of like discussing good horsemanship. Although I enjoy discussing horsemanship from an intellectual perspective and therefore discuss it quite a bit, I also feel that every year my ability increases and my interest in discussing it decreases perhaps a bit and I'm more interested in just riding.

*The only way to discover the limits of the possibilities*
*is to go beyond them into the impossible.*

—Arthur C. Clarke,
author

As a late-blooming rider, there have been times when just loping my horse seemed like stretching my limits into the impossible. The second horse that I started "myself" was such a forgiving, willing mare that she has allowed me great confidence to push myself beyond what I thought were my limits. Now, with my third horse just under saddle, those boundaries keep getting pushed further and further out. If I had a couple more lifetimes, I can't imagine how far I could get!

————

*Action should culminate in wisdom.*

—from the *Bhagvadgita*
by M.K. Ghandi and Narahari D. Parikh

If I do something with my horse that doesn't turn out quite as I had planned, I at least want to learn something from it. For instance, one day I was working with my mare in my new round pen. She was perhaps five at the time, and always a pretty calm, willing horse. I had my lariat out and was solidifying her ability to tolerate a rope around her, which I had worked on quite a bit. But not enough, I found out...

I put it around her girth area and worked her around the pen. She moved quite comfortably. Then I moved it a little farther along her barrel and she was fine. So I took what I thought was the next step and, while she was moving out, moved the lariat to her flank area and snugged it up a little. Well, as they say, all hell broke loose. My calm little mare was disturbed enough by this to crash around and get a hind leg outside the pen—I felt extremely lucky that she did no more physical harm to herself than skin her leg a little.

Sometimes what you think is the next step may need a few steps in between. Always take the extra steps for the sake of your horse, even if you think you can handle the results of the bigger steps. For instance, I could have first put the lariat around my mare's flank at a standstill, then at a walk perhaps on the end of the leadrope first so I could help control any fear response she may have. If ultimately you don't need those smaller steps, you will get through them quickly anyway so it's worth taking the time.

*Heaven and hell is right now. You make it heaven or you make it hell by your actions.*

—George Harrison,
musician

You can take a mistake you did or a problem you are having with your horse and you can work yourself and your horse up over it, making life hell for the both of you. Some issues with your horse can be quite serious and dangerous and of course you shouldn't ignore them. But nitpicking will make both of you crazy!

*Anger is only one letter short of danger.*

—Anonymous

Managing anger is a key element of good horsemanship. There are perhaps a half dozen horsemen in the world, I suspect, whose knowledge is at a high enough level that they don't get angry with their horses once in a while. I admit I still get angry when I am riding my mare and I feel she is doing something that is just "irrational" based on our past experiences. And I get angry with my horses when they do things like crowd me when I am feeding—things I feel that I have taught them are not acceptable and they "know better" than to be doing.

But the big difference that I have been able to reach is that my anger only lasts a couple of seconds—and I am usually more annoyed than actually angry—and even when I have to be pretty forceful with a horse to get my point across, I certainly don't hold a grudge. Instead, I look more to where I can increase the level of feel I have for horses in order to avoid all together these things that make me angry.

—————

*How many things there are which I do not want.*

—Socrates,
Greek philosopher

When I first re-entered the horse world after an equine-less decade, I had no equipment. I immediately began to accumulate things. Some things are necessary, like brushes and feed buckets and halters and leadropes. But the more clinics I went to, and the more I learned about good horsemanship, the less paraphernalia I collected. I learned that if I could teach myself to allow my horse a peaceful frame of mind, to allow my horse freedom of movement, and present myself to my horse in a way that is fitting to her and allows her to want to be with me, I wouldn't need all that stuff to confine my horses like nose chains and cross ties and tiedowns. If I could learn to be able to educate my horse to be particular about where he placed his feet when interacting with humans and human contraptions like horse trailers, I didn't much need leg wraps. And since one of the things I was learning about the most was to be as concerned with the mental horse as the physical horse, then that eliminated many things to be interested in buying. And now I walk through a large tack shop or an equine trade show and see so many things that I do not want.

*I've started so I'll finish.*

—Magnus Magnusson,
writer

Sometimes I've had to rethink my idea of "finishing," but even then it's important that there is some kind of "wrap up" to whatever you start with your horse. And one of the important and perhaps difficult things I've learned is how to realize that the best finish point may be way sooner than I was thinking it would be!

A friend came to my place with her teenaged mare and provided moral support to both me and my newly started filly to go on a little trail ride through our woods. Typically, when I get back, I ride over to the barn entrance to get off. But when we got near the house I could see that the furnace repairman had arrived. I decided to get off my filly way before we got to the bulkhead—we had had such a nice little ride that I could envision it ending poorly if the furnace repairman appeared from the bulkhead just as we were walking by it to the barn. I made the "finish" to our ride a little sooner than I'd planned because I thought it would make more of a chance that I would successfully finish what I started.

*The time is always right to do what is right.*

—Martin Luther King, Jr.,
civil rights leader

The key to doing what is right is deciding what is "right" to begin with! If you are doing things with your horse that you deep down don't feel good about, then you probably need to examine what you feel is right about interacting with horses.

*Progress always involves risk; you can't steal second base and keep your foot on first.*

—Frederick Wilcox

One of the things I have appreciated most about the horsemanship approach I have chosen to be involved with these past ten years is the element of safety that it brings. The focus isn't on the issue of safety directly, but the things that I've learned to consider important—yielding, directing the feet, softness, supporting your horse—provide me with the tools to call on to avoid and recover from sticky situations. So now I can dare to take a risk, to try to progress by inching closer to that imaginary line that separates my horse and I from trouble. And if I brush too close to the line and things start to fall apart, I can pull out one of the tools in our increasingly reliable toolbox and get us both back within the safety zone. It's a good feeling, and definitely allows progress to happen by being comfortable to move that imaginary line farther and farther out.

*Never let yesterday use up today.*

—Richard H. Nelson

Whatever happened the previous day working with a horse is water over the dam. While each day does not exactly offer a clean slate and so previous work needs to be considered, when you are with your horse dwelling only on what has happened in the past is as useful as worrying about what happens to the refrigerator light when you close the door. With a more mindful approach, what is happening here and now is what matters.

*If there is to be any peace at all it will come through
being, not having.*

—Henry Miller,
author

Good handling can be accomplished with nothing more
than a halter and a lead rope, and good horsemanship can be
accomplished with a simple snaffle bit bridle and a good saddle
("English" or "Western" is a non-issue). I choose to spend my
time and money on going to clinics, both as a spectator and a
participant, conducted by people from whom I would like to
learn. I am more interested in the "being" of horses—educating
myself to be able to educate my horses and give both of us the
best chance for communicating—and not "having" stuff. I have
plenty of fun buying the basics and that just that keeps my wal-
let smoking!

*Even a mistake may turn out to be the one thing necessary to a worthwhile achievement.*

—Henry Ford,
auto manufacturer

Well, I have my third in a succession of F-150 pickups sitting in the yard and its companion is a Ford Explorer, so it's pretty evident to me what Henry Ford was able to achieve despite or because of his mistakes! Although I always think about the long-term consequences of mistakes I've made, I finally had to stop worrying about making mistakes with my horses. If I do everything the best that I can then everything works out to the best of my ability. If I constantly work on trying to improve my ability, then every subsequent horse I work with should benefit from every previous mistake I made.

*The counsels of old age give light without heat, like the sun in winter.*

—Marquis de Vauvenargues

$\mathcal{O}$f all the clinics I have attended, it is the ones run by the clinicians that have been quietly conducting clinics around the country for years that seem the most calm. Perhaps it's not that they are less enthusiastic than the clinicians newer to the scene—all of the clinicians who are in it for the horse are extremely enthusiastic when they see something good happening for the horse. But with experience, and perhaps therefore age, does seem to come an ability to more easily ignore some of the stuff that might cause a little more fury in a younger, less experienced person. Perhaps in anything we do, when we find a "counsel" that we admire, we should also trace back to who their teacher was and find out more about that winter sun.

*We never do anything well till we cease to think about the manner of doing it.*

—William Hazlitt,
essayist

Sometimes, instead of analyzing our actions with our horses, and our horses' actions, perhaps we should just ride.

*The path to success is to take massive, determined action.*

—Anthony Robbins,
motivational speaker

After a summer of encountering barn sourness in my mare on the trails through our own woods, I become totally weary of her bratty behavior. At one point when things were getting on the border of being dangerous, I decided the degree of her behavior needed to be matched with a like degree of "determined action" from me. I am not proud to admit I got a little angry but I was desperate to get beyond this.

After this particular session, she got very forward and we had a nice ride. It didn't "cure" her but every time we rode our own trails thereafter her fits were shorter in duration and less dramatic, and I always matched my reaction to the level of her actions.

———·•·———

*[Humans are] the only animal that can be bored.*

—Erich Fromm,
psychoanalyst

I actually do think horses can get bored, although I don't imagine that they think of it as that. They surely don't stand around thinking "Man, I'm so bored, I have to find something to do." They are doing what they are doing at any given moment. However, the nomadic nature of the horse probably means that if they aren't able to move around much during the day, they may become what humans call bored.

*Dullness is the coming of age of seriousness.*

—Oscar Wilde,
playwright

Perhaps when we get too "serious" with our horses is when we make them dull! Maybe if we got serious from the start, we wouldn't have to get "too" serious to begin with. By that I mean if I want my horse to move and I indicate that with my seat but he doesn't move, so I bump once with my legs and he doesn't move, and then I bump a few more times and he moves just a little, until finally I'm urging with my seat, bumping with my legs, and whacking him on the flank with a crop or mecate all at the same time—well, that's "too" serious an amount of urging! Perhaps if I got better about being serious up front—the best deal followed by the deal that gets the preferred action—then my horse would learn pretty quickly that I was serious the first time around and I would never have to get "too" serious and make him dull.

*The puzzle of the round pen is that you go there to work
your horse so you can stop going there to work your
horse.*

—from the text of *Straight West*
by Verlyn Klinkenborg,
photography by Lindy Smith

This quote makes me think of my expensive, sturdy round
pen sitting prominently at the entrance to our farm's lower
driveway. It sits mostly idle but I wouldn't be without it. The
round pen is now in between having helped me start two of my
horses. My filly and I are still at the stage where all of our rides
at least begin in the round pen, but there will come a time in the
next year or so where we will once again abandon the round
pen. And just so the round pen doesn't get rusty, I recently
bought a yearling colt…

*Even a stopped clock is right twice a day.*

—Marie von Ebner-Eschenbach,
author

This quote gives me a little support when I begin to think that everything I do with my horse isn't working. Something has to be going right, even if by default! Perhaps a good first step is to sharpen my awareness enough to notice these two times a day when the "clock" is right.

*The glory of success is not in never falling, but in rising every time we fall.*

—Anonymous

We always hear how "important" it is if you fall off a horse to get right back on. Although it's probably inevitable if you ride horses that you will fall off sometime or another, it's important to assess why it is we fell off and at least if we fall off again, we can make sure it's not for the same reason!

*Millions long for immortality who don't know what to do with themselves on a Sunday afternoon.*

—Susan Ertz
from *Anger in the Sky*

Anyone who doesn't know what to do with himself or herself on any afternoon should get a horse! If you can't ride, you can do groundwork. If you can't do groundwork, you can groom. If you don't feel like grooming, there is manure to be picked up. If that doesn't appeal to you at the moment, there's a wheelbarrow to repair or a fence to mend. If you can't do that, there's brushes and saddle blankets to be washed. And if none of that is within the realm of possibilities at that moment, you can always spread out on the sofa and further your education with a horse book or magazine or dream with an equine catalog!

*Most people would succeed in small things, if they were not troubled with great ambitions.*

—Henry Wadsworth Longfellow,
poet

I long ago gave up the notion that I was ever going to accomplish even a thimbleful of the horsemanship of the people I admire the most. Instead of a feeling of defeat, this thought seemed to free me up to enjoy my own short list of horse accomplishments.

Most of the active horsemen who I admire don't put much stock in trying to put good horsemanship into words. But if horsemanship doesn't come naturally to me, writing does and writing about my experience learning a new way with horses has been extremely rewarding, helping me take on what I learn as my "own" and helping me better understand what I am attempting to learn.

Just understanding my own level of success has been for me a small success of its own.

*In the face of an obstacle which is impossible to overcome, stubbornness is stupid.*

—Simone de Beauvoir,
author

I suspect with horses no obstacle is completely impossible to overcome, but it may be impossible for me, at my skill level, to overcome. That means I not only need to be aware of my own skill level, but I need to accept it (while always trying to improve it). When I come across obstacles that seem impossible for me, I find help from someone for whom it would be possible.

*Animals are such agreeable friends—they ask no
questions, they pass no criticisms.*

—George Eliot,
author

As some who always has a couple sheep, goats, horses,
dogs, cats, and more hanging around the property, I do enjoy
the friendship and company of animals. Sometimes it is frustrating when I want to travel and can't find a housesitter, but the
few times that this happens does not outweigh the pleasure I get
from them the rest of the time.

*They demanded that people be disciples, not just learners.*

—Milton Friedman (economist)
discussing Ayn Rand (writer)
and Ludwig van der Rohe Mieses (architect)

I have always enjoyed reading Ayn Rand, it's hard not to admire someone who believes in something so thoroughly as Rand did her philosophy of objectivism even if I don't believe in the philosophy itself. However, I do not tend to be the sort who would be a disciple.

But sometimes going to as many clinics each year as I do makes me feel like I am a disciple. I just like to take the opportunity to learn from people I admire since I have so much to learn about horses.

*A horse rides the way it's ridden.*

—from *Riding Freedom*
by Pam Muñoz Ryan

A friend of mine one day brought up the question of why, when things aren't working out, I don't feel that some of the responsibility belongs to the horse. I am still pondering that comment, but for now I continue to believe that how things go when I ride my horses is almost exclusively my fault—good or bad. As my timing and awareness—and, with a little help from regular chiropractic adjustments, my seat—has gotten better over the years, I have definitely felt my riding improve. And my horse has become easier to ride, and she didn't have to do anything, she just better understood what I was asking of her because I got more clear in my ability to ask it. She is not the one who came to me and said "would you please confine me in a rocky excuse for a pasture by day, put me in a small corral at night, and throw a saddle on me a few times a week and take me away from my two horse friends." Until she does ask me to be ridden, I feel that I need to take full responsibility for our communication.

*It's kind of fun to do the impossible.*

—Walt Disney, film producer

When I decided I wanted an Arabian as my next project, I did chuckle when a friend said "You know about Arabians, don't you?" While I believe that ultimately a horse is a horse is a horse, I also realize that different breeds have different characteristics. So yes, I "know about Arabians" having the reputation of being flighty and a bit wired-for-sound in the "undesireable traits" column along with a huge list of desireable traits. To be honest, I mostly, after three Quarter Horses in my life, wanted a skinny horse for my aching hips.

I'd also heard many people express the idea that this approach to handling horses that I'd been studying for years works well mostly on stock type horses because they tended to be calm and good natured anyway. When an 18-month-old Arab sort of fell into my lap, I got to work on testing whether I was expecting impossible results starting her the way I'd started my last Quarter Horse mare a few more years of learning under my belt.

Cleo was started under saddle at a clinic when she was three, and the conclusion I've drawn is that while she is definitely a different personality type than my Quarter Horse mare (and so is my Quarter Horse gelding), Cleo has readily learned to respect my space, to operate from a yielding frame of mind, and, after months of groundwork together, accepted saddle, and rider, and bit, and all else just as trustingly and as forgiving of my inadequacies as my Quarter Horse mare did.

*Experience is a great advantage. The problem is that
when you get the experience, you're too damned old to
do anything about it.*

—Jimmy Connors,
tennis player

Now that I am in my mid-forties, having spent a decade
barely scratching the surface of developing feel with horses, I try
not to think about how many riding years I may realistically
have left. Luckily, I have a few acquaintances who are riding well
into their seventies. And the most comforting thing is that even
if I can't ride at some point, I love simply watching horses and
hopefully I can do that forever.

*A man in a passion rides a horse that runs away with him.*

—Thomas Fuller,
author

Horses are sensitive and seem to feed off their riders' attitude and bearing. Riders who are a little on the hyperactive side would probably help themselves and their horses to find ways to calm down before riding, like doing yoga or meditating, or simply breathing or stretching exercises.

*It's a good rule in life never to apologize. The right sort of people do not want apologies, and the wrong sort take a mean advantage of them.*

—P.G. Wodehouse,
author

J put horses in the "right sort of people" category. Apologies mean nothing to a horse, they want right action to begin with. If we always approach our horses with the best intentions, apologies are probably unnecessary. An apology covers the past and horses live strictly in the present.

*The most solid stone in the structure is the lowest one in the foundation.*

—Kahlil Gibran,
writer

Whenever anything in the education of my horses starts to fall apart, I go back to the very basics of groundwork. In fact, my hypersensitive gelding and I always seem to be going back to the groundwork stage.

The good news is that the lowest stone in his foundation—the groundwork—is pretty solid and he is mostly easy to have around so our good groundwork has ensured his life as an ornament in my pasture.

*When a dog runs at you, whistle for him.*

—Henry David Thoreau,
naturalist

Maybe Thoreau's advice is simply an attempt to not get bitten by the dog running toward him! But it does seem to have some logic—attempting to make a potentially bad situation work out ok by simply going with the flow. If your horse isn't going where you want her to go, maybe simply going where she's going means you could have a good ride instead of a frustrating one.

*My horses understand me tolerably well; I converse with them at least four hours every day....they live in great amity with me and friendship to each other.*

—from *Gulliver's Travels*
by Jonathan Swift

If we can present ourselves well enough to our horses for them to understand us "tolerably well," then we're probably getting along fine.

*The wisest person is not the one who has the fewest failures, but the one who turns failures into best account.*

—Richard R. Grant

As I've mentioned, my "unrideable" (by me) teenaged gelding Bud is a daily reminder of a huge horse "failure" of mine. But as a two-year-old, he was the impetus for searching for a way to interact with horses with mutual respect as the goal. Without him I may never have started down the path to seeking my own good horsemanship. So now I don't tend to think of him as a failure but more as a point of comparison making almost all of my other horse projects appear extremely successful!

*Mama exhorted her children at every opportunity to
"jump at de sun." We might not land on the sun, but at
least we would get off the ground.*

—Zola Neale Hurston,
author

When I tell friends that I am off to a clinic and part of what
we are going to be learning is how to work cows from horseback, they look at me like I'm crazy. Many of my riding friends
comment that they would have no use for working cows. Well,
neither do I, technically; I don't have a cow on the property. But
for me—your basic pleasure rider—learning to work a cow is a
small version of "jumping at de sun."

In the clinics I attend and the level of cow working that I
get to, it really has nothing to do with cows at all. But while my
horses and I are learning how to work the cow we are not only
refining our ability to communicate, it also becomes clear why it
is important to be able to direct your horse's feet, to be precise
in your riding, and to teach your horse what all this means.
Whether the cow gets back to the herd or not is a clear measure
of how precise you and your horse have become.

*To learn you have to listen, to improve you have to try.*

—Anonymous

One of the problems that has arisen in the years that I've been attending clinics at the local facility is that quite a group of us have become friends and the clinics have become as much social events as anything. That makes listening difficult since we have a hard time not chitchatting when we are on the sidelines! I have traveled quite a bit to clinics in other parts of the country where I know no one and can sit and watch with no distractions.

But to really improve with my horsemanship, I have definitely had to get out there on my horse and try what is being taught, both in clinics and at home. It is completely different to understand something intellectually and to be able to accomplish it with my horse. And the good thing about being in the clinic as a riding participant, I'm not chatting with my friends but concentrating pretty hard on what I am trying to learn!

*...fear is instinctive...and requires no conscious thought.*

—from "Animal Emotions" by Laura Tangley,
*U.S. News and World Report* 10/30/00

Anyone who has been around horses at all knows that it takes very little to provoke what we assume to be fear in horses. Even my most solid horse, who is far from "finished" but is well beyond green broke and has been exposed to lots of different situations, jumps almost every time we pass our wood pile where chipmunks scatter into crevices as we approach.

The instinct to be fearful and ready to bolt still seems to be right there on the surface. As we give our horses more experience to draw on, as they gain experience and exposure just by getting older, and as they learn that we can provide them with some support and assurance that things will be okay, that fear thing doesn't really seem to recede from the surface—it is still right there when they feel threatened—it just doesn't seem to be called upon as often.

This is why I get discouraged when I see horses advertised as "bombproof." To use that term to imply a guarantee that a horse will not react in fear is simply bad judgment—every horse has some line that can be crossed to cause them to react fearfully. A horse that may be "bombproof" to one person may not be bombproof at all when it gets to a new owner who cannot offer the level of support and comfort to the horse that its previous rider did.

*The ability to focus attention on important things is a defining characteristic of intelligence.*

—from *Irrational Exuberance*
by Robert J. Shiller

Many people say that a young horse has a very short attention span. Buck Brannaman has often pointed out in clinics of his that I have attended that, in the course of time that he works with a young horse in the round pen, the horse never once was not paying attention to the fact that Buck was in the pen with him, but the attention of the people around the outside of the round pen had been lost numerous times. I don't know what that says about the defining characteristic of human intelligence compared to horses…

*I do want to get rich but I never want to do what there
is to do to get rich.*

—Gertrude Stein, author

To get rich working with horses, whether it is doing clinics or preparing other people's horses for shows or simply training a young horse to be ridden, would require doing things in a way that are not in the horse's best interests. If the horse's education is hurried or compromised just because it is financially expedient, the horse is the one that suffers for it. Ultimately, the horse's owner loses too since horses cannot be rushed beyond their individual abilities and it will show up in later years.

The best way to enjoy horses and make the best life for them is to care about becoming rich in your horsemanship and skills and awareness, not in monetary ways.

*Tell me thy company and I'll tell thee what thou art.*

—Miguel de Cervantes,
writer

A version of this quote might be "show me a person's horse and I will tell thee what they art." Our horses tell a lot about what we are since the horse reflects their handling and the way they live. Although being calm and avoiding being neurotic around horses won't guarantee that they act calmly and not be neurotic, it does help considerably.

*If you want to conquer fear, don't sit home and think about it. Go out and get busy.*

—Henry Wadsworth Longfellow,
poet

To conquer fear of riding, we need to ride. It doesn't mean we need to put ourselves in dangerous situations. If we ride enough in situations that do not cause us to be fearful, we will eventually get bored and we will push our boundaries a little.

For instance, perhaps I am most comfortable riding my horse in circles in an indoor arena but add anything to the mix—obstacles, other riders, etc.—and I get less comfortable. So I will probably tend to ride in circles in the indoor over and over and over. Eventually, this will bore both me and my horse. Suddenly, another rider in the arena makes things a tad more interesting for both of us. Maybe I learn to relax about it by chatting with the other rider and commiserating over "problems" we are experiencing with our horses. Then maybe the other rider and I decide to put down a few cross rails. Before you know it, by simply "getting busy" I will have pushed my boundaries to something even more drastic like riding on a trail or loading my horse in a trailer and going to a different arena to ride for a couple hours!

*Continuous efforts—not strength or intelligence—is the key to unlocking our potential.*

—Winston Churchill,
British Prime Minister

J've never quite known what "potential" is, but I realized almost immediately upon embarking on this new journey with horses ten years ago that if I relied on my strength to get me through, I'd be done with horses inside a week. My wits could help—more common sense than intelligence—but without the "continuous effort" that Churchill mentions here, wits nor intelligence nor common sense were going to get me anywhere.

So off to clinics I go, every chance I can, every one I can afford. Riding, watching, whatever. And just when I think my spirits can't get any lower about my lack of ability, I take on a new project. There's nothing like a snappy young horse to remind you of the value of continuous effort. No matter what sticking points I have with my older horses, youngsters remind me that the horses that have come before them do show some results of good work and in a little while, maybe longer than someone else might take, the new horse will come along too.

————

*A mind troubled by doubt cannot focus on the course of victory.*

—from *Memoirs of a Geisha*
by Arthur Golden

$O$ne thing, among many, that has impressed me about the handful of clinicians I most admire is that when they begin to work with a horse they seem to be totally confident that they are going to accomplish whatever it is they set out to do with that horse. I have been able to emulate that attitude on a smaller scale by learning to approach larger goals by breaking them down into smaller steps—exactly what I've been taught to do with the horse works for me too. So even if the greater goal seems unattainable, if my steps toward it are small enough to allow me to be successful, this builds my confidence while building toward the larger goal.

*He doth nothing but talk of his horse.*

—from *Hamlet*
by William Shakespeare

All horse people know how true this quote can be when you get a group of us together. But when you really begin to refine your relationship with your horses, it becomes so astonishing that it is hard not to talk about them with everyone!

*From a certain point onward, there is no longer any
turning back. That is the point that must be reached.*

—Franz Kafka,
author

For the first several years after I rekindled my interest in horses
and began to learn an approach completely new to me, I felt like
a complete fraud. During that time, I rode only with horse
friends of like mind, a group of people I met at clinics I attended.

I probably avoided "venturing out" at first because I was not
confident of my ability. But eventually I realized that I had
learned enough to be able to be true to the approach I was
learning, that I could even go so far as to take lessons and ride
lesson horses the way the instructor told me to even though it
was a way (short reins, tight nosebands, etc.) that I would never
ride my own horses. I could take from the lesson what worked
for me and my approach to horses, and leave the rest behind. It
is a good feeling, to trust my own knowledge.

*There are two things for which animals can be envied:*
*they know nothing of future evils, or of what people say*
*about them.*

—Voltaire

As much as we humans feel we have so much at our disposal, I often think how fortunate animals are that things like weather reports hold no meaning for them. When it turns colder, it does, and their bodies adjust as necessary in response not in anticipation. They don't hang around fretting over whether that storm will actually come up the coast or veer off to sea. It is nice to be able to make preparations, but sometimes I feel it might be nice once in a while to just experience things when they come.

*I think if the horse wants to be somewhere else while I
am working with him, my efforts are a waste of time.*

—Joe Wolter from "Another Approach"
in *America's Horse* Nov/Dec 2000

For the horse to have a good attitude and to want to be with
you while you are working with him, it seems to me that you
have to be sure your horse finds you reliable in your
approach. He has to want to be with you because he trusts
you, respects you, and he knows you respect him. He can't be
fearful of what your next move is going to be or confused
about whether he did what you wanted him to or not. If he's
confident in your relationship, if you have proven yourself
consistently reliable, he will try and understand what you
want even if it is confusing at first. And when he's thinking,
and trying, and feeling ok about being with you, he doesn't
think about being somewhere else.

## JULY 7

———•••———

*A lot of people have trouble catching a horse. But when he gets ready to catch, it's simple.*

—Ray Hunt in *The Trail Less Traveled*

$\mathcal{A}$ while back, I became accidentally involved in catching a horse in her paddock who was new and not interested in being caught to come in for the evening. The person who was trying to catch the horse had many other things to do and was happy to let me take over and try some of the techniques I was just beginning to learn.

I put pressure on the horse when she turned away from me and backed off and was still when her attention was on me. In around ten minutes, I felt like I was making progress enough to have the horse ready to be caught pretty soon. But someone decided things weren't developing fast enough for him, and he showed up a long whip. The horse got a crack with the whip every time she got close enough in the somewhat narrow paddock. When I started to walk out to get away from what was shaping up, the horse rushed up to me. I grabbed her halter, handed her to the man with the whip, and reminded myself never to get involved in anything like that again.

Maybe the whip method worked since the horse sure was interested in getting out of that pen. But I choose to think that what I had started was working and amidst the confusion the horse came to me because she decided that I was as close to a friend as she was going to get at that moment; that we had developed a glimmer of communication that she decided was worth capitalizing on right about now.

*If you want to succeed, you must make your own opportunities as you go.*

—John B. Gough,
public speaker in 1800s

J read recently about someone who built a round pen with solid sides so her horses wouldn't get distracted by things going on outside the pen while she was working with them. But if working with a horse in a round pen is in part to help your horse become focused on you and the work you are doing together, what have you accomplished if the horse has nothing else to focus on anyway? It seems to me the opportunity you might set up in a round pen is to have lots of distractions but use the round pen to help your horse learn that the important thing while you are in the pen with him is to pay attention to you, not the things going on outside the pen. If you don't allow this, you miss a great opportunity for learning and success.

*The great enemy of creativity is fear. When we are fearful, we freeze up—like a nine-year-old who won't draw pictures, for fear everybody will laugh. Creativity has a lot to do with a willingness to take risks.*

—Faith Ringgold
in *Fast Company* magazine

My fear of being "creative" with my horses comes from my average riding ability. The better my riding has become over the years, the more risks I've been willing to take because I have a little more confidence that things will turn out ok. I have worked hard to increase my riding ability, taking lessons on school horses and getting pushed beyond my comfort level, riding in clinics to work with my own horses, buying saddles that fit my horse appropriately and make me feel secure, and riding as many different horses as possible. And just riding as often as possible, that's the real key!

*We are more inclined to hate one another for points on which we differ than to love one another for points on which we agree.*

—Charles Caleb Colton

In spreading my wings a little and riding with people who don't share my philosophy about horses, I do find this quote to be true. I don't know about the "hate" part, but I do definitely end up talking more with these people about the differences of our thinking than any similarities we might have. It's frustrating to me and something I don't feel I have made much progress changing. However, I have chosen not to simply avoid riding with people who think differently about horses than I do, which I guess is a step in the right direction.

*It is necessary to make sure that the horse does not
become spoiled when he is first started in the bridle.
If it is not done right, he can acquire a lot of bad habits
which will be very hard to overcome later on.*

—from *Reinsman of the West,*
by Ed Connell

Many other people don't seem to mind, but I will not tolerate a horse grabbing onto the leaves of branches along the trail
or ripping the reins out of my hands to dive for grass while
crossing a meadow. It seems dangerous to have your saddle
horse so focused on when the next snack is coming into reach
that he isn't paying much attention to what you're asking of him.

It's like allowing your kids to walk through the grocery eating off the shelves as they go—why is it acceptable for a 1,000-
pound animal to do the same? Riders whose horses do this clearly
don't like the behavior since they are always grumbling at the
horse and pulling on his mouth in vain trying to get him to stop.
It can't be better to pull on the horse's mouth several times over
the course of a ride than to simply do what it takes to make him
think twice about ever eating on the trail again.

Easier, of course, is to be sure the behavior is never learned
in the first place, but unless you always get young, unstarted
horses you have to deal with what you've got.

*No matter how old a mother is, she watches her*
*middle-aged children for signs of improvement.*

—Florida Scott-Maxwell
in *The Measure of My Days*

$\mathcal{O}$nce or twice a year for ten years I would get it in my head
to stick my now-teenaged gelding in the round pen and see if
age had changed anything to make him more rideable. It never
had and I finally realized that I was the one who had to change.

*Horse sense is the thing a horse has which keeps it from betting on people.*

—W.C. Fields,
actor

*O*ne of the things I love about the approach to horsemanship I have been studying over the years is that it provides a real standard against which I measure all I do with my horses. If the benefit is to the horse and the horse's understanding, then it seems to fit my philosophy. If it is something that is just addresses the physical or is to benefit the human more than the horse, it probably isn't suitable to me.

—·—·—

*Boredom is simply the lack of imagination.*

—Julie O. Smith

J can ride around twenty minutes in circles in an arena before I am ready to spice things up a bit. This is where imagination can help. Out comes a tarp, a flag, ground rails, anything that is available. And if there's nothing around that can serve as props, I might work at getting my horse to like that scary corner better than anywhere else in the arena, or how precisely I can back circles. This makes it hard to ride in most public indoor arenas since many riders focus on rail work and typically don't like one person riding all around the arena in a disorderly fashion.

*Pick battles big enough to matter, small enough to win.*

—Jonathan Kozol,
writer

J've learned a lot in the past few years about breaking things down for the horse when trying to teach her something. The steps have to be big enough that she can make some sense of what I am asking her to do but small enough that she can actually be successful at it. This feeling of accomplishment, even in small increments, is great for the both of us. But I have finally learned to avoid "battles" as much as possible.

*It had long since come to my attention that people of accomplishment rarely sat back and let things happen to them. They went out and happened to things.*

—Elinor Smith

Just waiting for things to come up to expose your horse to won't move your horse's education along much. You can't recreate or experience everything, but if you never leave your dooryard or the riding arena, you definitely won't come upon anything new. The key is learning things in the arena or round pen like disengaging the hindquarters or softness that will allow you to keep yourself safe and your horse safe when you head for some exposure.

*Worry lives a long way from rational thought.*

—Mary Roach
in *Self* magazine

Horses express worry in different ways, just like humans. Become aware of how your horse expresses worry—wrinkles around the eyes, a slight sweat, moving around a lot. Prove yourself worthy of being the one your horse can look to when he is anxious; when something of concern comes up, the horse can react to your reaction and think rationally, which can help a potentially dangerous situation work out ok, or even just get you by a garbage can at the end of a driveway!

*Riding is an act of persistent self-criticism.*

—Verlyn Klinkenborg,
writer

I never have been very flattering of my own riding skills. Over a decade into my rekindled interest in horses, I have finally realized that I ride better than I think I do. But in order to keep getting to be better riders, we do constantly have to keep assessing our current skill level and the horses seem to test that skill level constantly. But we are, as the cliché goes, "our own worst critics" so maybe we seek riding instruction because we know our instructor will never be as critical as we are of ourselves!

*All animals, except man, know that the principal
business of life is to enjoy it—and they do enjoy it as
much as man and other circumstances will allow.*

—Samuel Butler,
satirist

The horse's idea of enjoyment of life can be quite different
from the human's idea of it. Horses may not "enjoy" being ridden but they do seem to thrive on being busy, logically harken-
ing back to their nomadic roots where in the wild they are
always on the search for food and on the lookout for predators.
It seems pretty safe to say that horses are typically not enjoying
themselves when locked for long periods day after day in a stall,
no matter how cushy the stall seems to us humans.

*My goal is simple. It is complete understanding of the universe, why it is as it is and why it exists at all.*

—Stephen Hawking,
scientist

Like Hawking's goal with the universe, the goal of completely understanding the horse is most likely unreachable. But as unattainable as it may be, trying to completely understand the horse will certainly provide a lifetime of always having something to do.

*Sitting quietly, doing nothing, Spring comes, and the grass grows by itself.*

—from *The Gospel According to Zen*

*E*xcept for us having imposed ourselves on the horse as their food provider, horses can actually get through the day quite nicely without a human. My horses have an interesting little life of their own. When the sun comes up over the trees in the right spot, they arrange themselves for a sunny nap. Usually in late morning, they go over the hill and peck at the sparse grazing their turnout area has. They've designed a dusty area that is their rolling spot. When the day starts to turn hot, they head to a low area near the garden where the grass grows better and coolness comes up from the earth. They have their home well figured out and they go about their business for the day which only involves me when I arrive with food or a halter.

*The mind is like a parachute, it doesn't work unless it's open.*

—Anonymous

J have been accused of being closeminded to approaches outside the one I've discovered over the past ten years. Having never been called closeminded in my life, it certainly caused me to think a lot. Ultimately, I have come to the point of having enough understanding of the approach to horsemanship that resonates with me that I am pretty quickly able to recognize when something doesn't fit my overall outlook. However, something that I have started to learn more in the past couple years is to take what works for me from what I see in all approaches but I usually find that I apply it quite differently from the way it was presented to me. To get to that point took a lot of clinics and reading and talking and trying on my own horses to understand fully what I wanted to know in order to know when I was veering off that path. There are still some approaches whose fundamentals are just so distasteful to me that I cannot spend my time learning about them to know if there is anything in there for me or not. I can live with that.

*Live mindful of how brief your life is.*

—Anonymous

How many people in the world are privileged to interact everyday with horses as those of us who sacrifice other things to have horses? Spend time with your horse! Think about whether watching a television newsmagazine or shopping for plastic furniture at the local big-box store is really a more valuable use of your time.

*I have a simple philosophy. Fill what's empty. Empty what's full. Scratch where it itches.*

—Alice Roosevelt Longworth,
Theodore Roosevelt's daughter

Go into the round pen or arena or out on the trail with a plan in mind, but if something else comes up that seems to need attention don't just ignore it because that wasn't what you planned to work on this time. Expose your horse to new things and work on what comes of it. I spent quite a lot of time working with my mare on getting over being barn sour about riding out on the trails behind my house. But now that we are mostly beyond that, I don't expect everything to be perfect, I am always happy to work on things with my horses. If I wanted things to be the same every single time I'd ride my motorcycle instead of my horses.

*I think, what has this day brought me, and what have I given it?*

—Henry Moore,
sculptor

$\mathcal{E}$ven though my horsemanship skill level is not anywhere near where I would like it to be, every day I feel good about giving my horses a decent home and a safe and enjoyable life to the best of my ability. I am happy I care about things like my horses being respectful of me and at least trying to do what I am attempting to teach them. I am thankful that my pursuit of good horsemanship has brought me a life with horses and to give back, I work hard to better my skills.

*…love…unselfishness…integrity…sincerity…loyalty
to one's best…honesty…enthusiasm…humility…
goodness…happiness…fun. Practically every animal still
has these assets in abundance and is eager to share them,
given opportunity and encouragement.*

—J. Allen Boone
in *Kinship with All Life*

All of these attributes are important, but when working with horses (and many other things for that matter) the one that most resonates with me is honesty. If we approach our horses with honesty to the core—in our actions but most of all in our intentions—we should be able to get through most days in a positive light.

*Even if a farmer intends to loaf, he gets up in time to get an early start.*

—Edgar Watson Howe

 I love this quote! It has been years since I've been able to imagine "sleeping in" and it's fine with me. Early morning is my best time of the day—even in the rural area where I live it gets pretty noisy by around 7:00 AM with cars whooshing by as people head to work, school buses cranking along, heavy equipment grinding past headed to the newest house site or delivering gas and oil. I don't have to push myself to get out of bed in the morning to enjoy this peaceful time.

*Life is a succession of moments. To live each one is to succeed.*

—Sister Corita Kent,
artist

Success is a concept that each of us needs to define for our-selves. I have one horse who has been too much for me and I have not been able to ride. I could look at that as a failure, and I admit sometimes I do. But he is very nicely halter broken—soft, responsive, polite on the end of a lead rope—so I've had to learn to take my success with him where I can get it. Just recently I have had some successful rides on him and even within those rides I've had to take my successes in this succession of moments. But then, in a moment when fear took over completely, he ran me over to get out of his stall away from whatever he perceived as life threatening—I took that fact that I was alive and my head didn't get stepped on as a success... I continue to work on increasing his respect level and his ability to find support in me, but this horse has such a high level of self-preservation that I have not yet been able to adjust to suit him but only grab small moments of success.

*Your big opportunity may be where you are right now.*

—Napoleon Hill,
writer

If you always work on increasing your awareness, you will be more likely to recognize that what you are looking for may be right under your nose. If you are frustrated that your horse won't calm down on the trail and is more responsive to the other horses than to you, your opportunity to really make a difference is now. Use the energy the horse has, do some serpentines on the trail (no trail is too narrow to be able to weave even just a little) and while you are using up some of that energy in a positive way still moving forward, you are also working on getting your horse more responsive to your legs and hands. Right now is more useful than hanging on as best you can and waiting to work on it later in the ring when it won't hold much meaning to the horse.

*There is no such thing as a horse you can "just get on and ride."*

—Anonymous

People who sell horses get countless requests for a horse your can "just get on and ride." Why would people think this kind of horse even exists and if it did why anyone would want a horse like that anyway? The so-called "push-button horse" would take something that is a living, breathing, thinking animal and make a machine out of it.

Of course, what people really are wishing for is a safe horse that doesn't have bad habits while being ridden. But even if you purchase a horse that is like that for its current owner, you as the new person interacting with this horse will have to make the effort to keep it going. A good horse can develop bad habits pretty fast in the hands of a rider that doesn't want to think while riding. For those who want a "just-get-on-and-ride" horse, their money is probably better spent popping quarters into the metal steed in front of the grocery store.

*A wild beast may wound your body but an evil friend will wound your mind.*

—Buddha (Siddhartha Gautama,
founder of Buddhism)

It's easy to focus on the physical horse. It is something we can readily see—if the horse won't hold a desired position, there's always a tie-down or noseband to strap on and tighten to make them take up that physical position. Even drugs and herbs influence the physical brain, but not the thought process. If you get to your horse's mind, then you are really getting somewhere.

*Horsemen have always been susceptible to one great foible, and that is the belief that the categories and terms and concepts they apply to their art are ones that their horses hold, too.*

—from *The Nature of Horses*
by Stephen Budiansky

The sooner we let go of the idea that horses think like humans, the sooner we will start to make headway with our relationships with horses.

———— ‧ ————

*If the human doing the praising is not respected by the horse, the praise has no value.*

—from *Influencing Horse Behavior*
by Dr. Jim McCall

When I watch someone work with a horse and they make an effort to say "good boy" or coo "good girl, I find it interesting and a bit puzzling. The horse, I figure, isn't being good or bad they are just being. Thinking I was alone in this feeling, I kept it to myself. But a clinician I recently had the privilege of riding with for the first time brought it up in his clinic. He explained that he found it odd that people do that, because it implies that there is an opposite, a deserved "bad boy." But to the horse, it all doesn't matter, it's what we are concocting for him to do. It's a hard thing to explain—I certainly think praising your horse can't be a bad thing but to me it seems lacking a certain fundamental of what we are asking of horses in the first place.

In other words, the horse is always right, always "good boy"; the horse is always doing what he thinks he should be doing based on how we are communicating with the horse. It really should be the human who is being praised when the horse does something we want because we have been able to actually communicate sufficiently for a horse to understand what the heck we are asking of it.

*Fear almost always arises—in horses as well as in people—from concern about what might happen, and much more rarely from what is happening.*

—from *For the Good of the Horse*
by Mary Wanless

This is mindfulness in its essence. If we ride in the moment instead of in the moments ahead, we may not be so fearful of what might happen and enjoy our ride more!

*The will to succeed is important, but what's even more important is the will to prepare.*

—Bobby Knight

I never in a million years thought that the controversial college basketball coach Bobby Knight would have anything to say that resonates with me, but this quote did. One place in my horsemanship where spending the time on preparation has really paid off for me is in the groundwork I have done with my youngsters before I ever ride them. I spent almost two years just doing groundwork with them with my two horses I got as yearlings before I started them under saddle. I am certain, especially as my skill increased, this made them much easier for me to teach about being ridden.

*Yielding to pressure is important, regardless of what you are doing with a horse.*

—Joe Wolter in "Another Approach"
from *America's Horse* July/August 2000

There is almost nothing you can think of with horses that yielding to pressure doesn't have a positive impact on: you can lead them quietly, you can direct them through a gate precisely either on the ground or from the saddle, you can tie them with confidence, you don't worry so much about them stepping on a lead rope, they may be more likely to avoid resisting if they get caught in something, they will stand quietly on the end of a lead rope if they feel no pressure asking them to move, they are easier to ride—the list is endless!

*Some people believe anything they are told providing it's whispered to them.*

—A Dell "cryptogram"
puzzle saying

J couldn't resist this one. We always think horses make big deals out of small things, but we humans sure have a way of blowing things out of proportion too! *The Horse Whisperer*—which produced a whole new industry segment in the horse world—was just an entertaining novel and movie. As a writer, I am glad author Nicholas Evans probably made some money from a novel. As a horse person, it was nice to go see a movie with horses as a central theme where the horses are wearing quality tack and aren't being yanked around with curb bits and tie downs. And some horses and horse people I respect got to make a little money and be involved in the telling of a tale relating to their way of life. End of story. When horse people pick the Horse Whisperer tag line up and use it to promote themselves, all I can say is Buyer Beware.

*Changing gears from time to time makes it possible for us to get into the habit of being aware and alive each moment.*

—from *Living the Simple Life*
by Elaine St. James

After a decade of riding in western saddles and attending clinics put on mostly by western cowboy-types, I decided to start "riding English" again. I bought an English saddle to poke around the yard with and tried to increase my skills by taking weekly hunter-jumper lessons. It was a refreshing break. Learning on school horses and doing things the way the barn does (tight nose bands, short reins) really increased my awareness level. A lot of it I didn't agree with, but since I rode the barn's school horses and the instructor was easy to learn from, I chose to absorb what held meaning for me and my riding and dismiss the rest as soon as I got off the horse. I learned a lot, got to ride different horses, and had a lot of fun with my group of fellow students!

*In your handling, seek a balance between firm
and gentle.*

—from *The Basics of Western Riding*
by Charlene Strickland

Gentle seems like it should always be the preferred method,
but if you aren't getting your point across perhaps firming up a
little is important too. There's nothing wrong with meaning
what you say; your horse will probably appreciate it too, just the
plain fact that you are clearly communicating rather than, in an
attempt to be "gentle," being wishy washy. And sometimes a
horse is just taking over, which is dangerous for the both of you
and disrespectful too.

*[The rider] needs to realize how the person's approach can assure the horse that he can have his self-preservation and still respond to what the person is asking him to do.*

—from *True Unity*
by Tom Dorrance

This has come up several times already but it bears repeating: the most important thing to a horse is to feel like he has his self-preservation. The best way he can feel that is if he has the ability to move. Not that you necessarily want him to move in a given situation, but it seems to help if the horse knows he can move if he really has to.

*The riding of a young horse is an excellent nerve tonic.*

—from *Training Young Horses to Jump*
by Geoffrey Brooke

Whew, having had all of my horses since they were young, this quote rings a real bell! And the one to prove it to me the most is my young Arab mare—she has been very accommodating so far in her short riding career but she definitely keeps me on my toes! Many times while riding her I have said to myself and aloud "Wow, I didn't know I could ride this fast."

*You hit homeruns not by chance but by preparation.*

—Roger Maris,
baseball player

Preparation can be the key to lots of things. You certainly
don't want to take a young horse on a trail ride at least until you
have put some of the features on the horse that you might
need—brakes, accelerator, and steering to name perhaps the
most important ones. Doing some of these in the round pen or
arena is a good start. I like then to get going on the trails close
to my house. The way our place is set up, a young horse can
stay within sight and sound of her pasture mates but still experience being in a woodsy environment and maneuvering stumps
and rocks and roots and low-hanging branches and uneven
ground just like she will on a longer trail ride. It helps take that
start you got on steering and build on it in a real environment.
You don't need a woods trail—I ride around my truck, the old
well, the big tree beside the barn, anything that gives you a
definitive thing to steer around can be a big help to a young
horse, all in preparation for heading out on the trails.

*Adventure today means finding one's way back to the silence and stillness of a thousand years ago.*

—Pico Iyer,
travel writer

There certainly seems no better way to get back to a thousand years ago than riding out on horseback. After reading the book *All the Pretty Horses*, I got that kid-like feeling of wanting to imitate the riding in the film. The next time I climbed on my mare we left the trail and went rambling through the brush. Even though the terrain was a classic New England early succession forest, I just said the word "arroyo" a few times and I felt like I was on a Mexican adventure!

*Confidence is not found in rigidity but rather in free, relaxed motion.*

—from *Yoga for Your Spiritual Muscles*
by Rachel Schaeffer

Being rigid on a horse is probably the fastest way to make you and the horse uncomfortable. It even looks uncomfortable. I have found that all the instruction in the world couldn't force me to be comfortable on a horse, I had to ride lots of horses and just begin to feel that free, relaxed motion.

*Trust your hunches. They're usually based on facts filed away just below the conscious level.*

—Dr. Joyce Brothers

You'd think I'd have learned to trust my hunches by now. Oh, it's not that I don't have them—geez, I probably should check her out on the ground first before I get on. Or hmmm, maybe he isn't quite ready for this rope around his flank. Or, wow, this person sounds sincere in his approach to horses but his horse isn't quite convinced, so maybe he's not someone to learn from. I'm just now beginning to listen to these hunches ahead of time instead of after a wreck with my horse or a disappointment with a human.

*True riding mastery can only be reached by the person
who, for years and years, has kept his mind open to new
ideas, and even he should always be prepared
to admit there is still much to be learned.*

—from *Riding Logic*
by Wilhelm Muesler

Keeping yourself open to new ideas is certainly an admirable
trait, but I feel the piece of information that is often not included
is that at some point you need to be using those new ideas to
build on things you have come to believe, not to always be starting your thought process from scratch.

*[Yoga] is not about becoming the blind follower of any-thing, but about assisting you on your own chosen path.*

—from *Yoga for Body, Breath, and Mind*
by A.G. Mohan

While many of us who have met through our frequent atten-dance at "natural horsemanship" clinics laugh about being part of a cult, I have been careful to avoid becoming a blind follower. I recognized what was being taught as the kind of relationship with horses that I always hoped was possible but didn't know how to achieve. But my own personal ability level and physical constraints (I'm short, not very flexible, have bad hips, didn't start riding until I was 15 years old then left the horse world for a dozen or more years only to start over again in my mid thirties—the list is endless as is everyone's!) meant that I began pretty early on to take the approach I was learning and mold it into my own experience and ability and follow my own "chosen path" under the guidance of those I had chosen as teachers.

*A man who rode good horses was usually a good man.*

—from *They Rode Good Horses*
by Don Hedgpeth

The old saying goes that people's pets resemble themselves, and often this seems the case with horses. Part of it is that people choose to surround themselves with animals who have traits that are appealing to them, which is usually traits similar to those the human possesses. And they also bring out certain traits in an animal by having those traits themselves—a nervous person can bring out the nervousness in a horse, the person who operates out of anger often brings out anger and rebelliousness in the horse. It's very interesting to watch people and their horses. I seem to have a strange mix in my four (which says something about me!!) but the horse I have the closest relationship with is a mare who is very laid back as long as she's getting her own way!

*The highest reward for a person's toil is not what they get for it, but what they become by it.*

—John Ruskin

This journey through horsemanship that I've been on for more than a decade has certainly changed how I think about a lot of things. It becomes evident in my day-to-day relationships that have nothing to do with horses, from work colleagues to family relationships to what I expect of myself.

*I not only use all the brains I have, but all I can borrow.*

—Woodrow Wilson,
28th U.S. President

Going to numerous clinics has been my way to borrow brain power. Of course, the clinician goes away in a few days but I also have many friends whom I've turned to for added intelligence. Without them, I wouldn't have gotten far with my horses.

*When we seek to discover the best in others, we somehow bring out the best in ourselves.*

—William A. Ward

Having attended numerous clinics by many different clinicians over the years, I have found that the clinicians that are most appealing to me are the ones who really know how to pick out the best in their students and build on that. At the same time, they are almost magically able to blend in helping the student with the "worst" but always keeping things positive.

For instance, say a rider has "bad hands," always bumping the horse's mouth and sending mixed messages through the reins. Instead of yelling at the student to fix their hands, the clinician might pick one thing about the student's riding that is smooth and build on that until, by the end of the clinic, the student has come to understand that smoothness needs to go straight through their hands to the reins. By focusing on the positive stuff to build on, the student never had to feel dumb or get defensive (sounds like good horse handling techniques too!). But the good clinician also isn't so gooey positive that it rings false. It is quite an art.

*Enjoy the little things, for one day you may look back
and realize they were the big things.*

—Robert Brault

The Henry James short story "The Beast in the Jungle" is about a man who spends his entire life expecting some big tragedy to happen to him and with that always in his mind is blinded to and avoids the good things in life, like falling in love and getting married, even though they are right in front of him. The big thing never happens and he lives his life depriving himself of all the good things for no apparent reason.

Look for the little things with your horse. That she leads well or he is good to be around in his stall or that he stands calmly while being saddled.

*Too much of a good thing is wonderful.*

—Mae West,
actress

$O$ne year I somehow had signed up for a lot of clinics. I worked hard with my gelding who is difficult for me, and I worked with my newly started filly.

The last clinic of the year was coming up and I was trying to decide which horse to bring. I realized I was exhausted and I opted to bring my "best" horse. Oh, she certainly isn't lacking for the need for refinement—but she is fun to ride, easy to load in a trailer, and is all around easy to travel with. I felt guilty about not getting in one more session with one of my other horses but I was ready for too much of a good thing and it turned out to be a really nice way to wrap up the "clinic season."

—·—

*…skate to where the puck is going to be, not where it has been.*

—Wayne Gretzky,
hockey player

This reminds me of always looking ahead to the next jump on a jump course. By the time you are lined up to go over a jump, your preparation for that one is long over and it's time to start preparing for the next one.

With horses, if you spend all your time focusing on the past you are never going to get to where you want to be—there is no way you will be lined up for the next jump if you are still riding the last one.

*A good horse is never a bad color.*

—cowboy saying and title of a book
by Mark Rashid

$\mathcal{E}$arly on in attending clinics I noticed this phenomenon about the attractiveness of certain horses. Horses that came into the round pen that were bothered in general, obnoxious to the clinician, and all around arrogant and disrespectful became more and more physically attractive as they changed mentally. By the time the clinic was over, the most mundane bay horse could be the most handsome horse in the clinic if it had let down mentally. The transformation isn't usually evident, it would come in the form of my thinking after the third day or so "geez, that horse is actually quite good looking."

*Exhilaration is that feeling you get just after a great idea hits you, and just before you realize what's wrong with it.*

—Unknown

Whenever I hit on a "great idea" for working with my horses, I run it by my horse mentor. I always find it helpful to get a different perspective and I can trust if my idea is really not very sound, she will pretty quickly see the holes and point them out. I am pretty sure this has saved me a few wrecks.

*There is more to life than increasing its speed.*

—Mohandas K. Gandhi

Cantering a horse is something that didn't come naturally to me. My bad hips may have something to do with it—I have had to spend a long time getting better seated and more capable of adjusting my position "on the fly" because it would take so much effort to get the horse to canter that by the time she did, I would be well out of position. My now-eight-year-old mare was six before we got it together enough for her to readily pick up a canter just by using my seat—but that's as long as we are on the trail. I still don't seem to be balanced enough to get her to canter in a more enclosed area like a round pen, although we are making a breakthrough in the arena.

For a long time I let this bother me. Finally, I decided cantering in the arena or round pen didn't matter, I didn't need to "increase my speed" for any particular reason at the moment. I know I can on the trail and we just keep working on the rest.

*I long to accomplish a great and noble task, but it is my
chief duty to accomplish small tasks as if they were great
and noble.*

—Helen Keller

Just dreaming about riding the Tevis Cup or an Olympic
cross country competition or, lately, the AQHA Versatility
Ranch Horse Competition has been good enough for me. Those
tasks may be greater than standing still while for mounting or
lining up to pick me up off the fence but these are great and
noble tasks in my book compared with "world-class equestrians"
I've seen who need to have two people hold their horse and a
third to help them climb aboard!

*A teacher affects eternity; he can never tell where his influence stops.*

—Henry Adams

A clinician I was listening to criticized other clinicians for using a flag in their clinics. This person felt that the others were encouraging people to use flags but the students would go away not really knowing how to use this tool and were, in fact, probably making more horses lives miserable than better. This kind of thing has certainly happened to the round pen—more and more round pens are being sold but most people buying them don't know how to use them for more than things they could probably simply accomplish with a lunge line. However, sometimes you need to gain as much knowledge as you can and then work it out for yourself so if the clinician never used things like flags and round pens I think most people and their horses would lose out.

*Genius does what it must, talent does what it can.*

—Edward Bulwer-Lytton

J'm neither a genius nor exceptionally talented so I guess I do what I enjoy!

*Every person is responsible for all the good within the scope of his abilities, and for no more.*

—Gail Hamilton

At some point in my pursuit of good horsemanship, I realized I can only rise to the level I am of my ability at any given time. But at the same time I can always be in pursuit of increasing my ability.

*...if you are thinking about your riding, you are interfering with your horse.*

—Buster in the essay
of the same name from
*Some Horses* by Thomas McGuane

Riding through feel, I think, comes from riding a lot and being able to feel when something is right or not right. Mechanics do of course come into play, they have to, and spending time working on your position is important. But always focusing on mechanics and thinking too hard about every little position of every one of your body parts will interfere with your riding—you can't understand what your whole body is feeling while your brain is otherwise engaged keeping track of where each leg is and how you are holding your fingers.

*It's very much a question of reinforcing choices as one makes them, of going further in and confirming them.*

—Muriel Rukeyser

For quite a few years I attended several clinics a year, usually to acquire new knowledge and work on specific things with my horses. But just as often, I am looking for confirmation that my choices with my horse have been good ones, that the direction I am going in is a good direction.

After a while I began to get this confirmation from a different approach—I branched out of the clinic group and rode with people who didn't come from the same horse world that I had immersed myself in. In this environment, I could see in my own horse or in looking at other people's horses that I was comfortable with my own choices. This is where I really began to realize how much I had learned (or not) over the years—I could look to the horse to let me know.

*The most exhausting thing in life is being sincere.*

—Anne Morrow Lindbergh,
author

A lot of hard work goes into truly caring about something. It's easy to be sincere on the surface, to say you care about something, like changing the behavior in your horse. But horses make it pretty clear that they know whether or not you are sincere. Until you are, be ready to do the hard work of changing your approach. To ask only the horse to change is not being sincere.

*Many things will catch your eye, a few will catch your heart—pursue these.*

—Anonymous

Most of us try out this or that hobby in our lives and we probably don't stick with all of them. I have loved to knit since I was a teenager and I love nice yarns and knitting needles and poring over sweater patterns. Once I had my own farm, I thought it logical to extend that love of knitting to keeping my own sheep and using their wool to make my yarn. I started with two, got up to eight, and now have several fleeces in my garage and no sheep in the barn. Unlike some people I met in my pursuit of this hobby, sheep and fleece and spinning just didn't resonate with me. It took me six years with sheep but finally I realized that I'd rather put my energy into what does fulfill my heart—giving a good home to horses and challenging myself to be mindful enough in my horsemanship to help my horses be respectful of humans and mentally sound enough to live a content life.

*And the picture of the true horse, what does that look like? That too depends—not on everything, but on who you allow yourself to be.*

—from the text of *Straight West*
by Verlyn Klinkenborg,
photography by Lindy Smith

*O*ur horses are who they are, but our lives together depend on us humans. By taking them under our care, we are accepting the responsibility for their lives and how they live that life is dependent on what we choose to teach them about human interaction.

*Somehow we learn who we really are and then live with that decision.*

—Eleanor Roosevelt,
First Lady

 $\mathcal{B}$ ecoming involved with horses is probably a major shortcut to learning who we really are. If your horse life is miserable and you've tried as hard as you can to change that, maybe horses are not for you. Maybe you only think they are your heart's desire— maybe you like all the tack and the other physical accoutrements of having a horse. Maybe you like the hustle and bustle of the show environment. Or you love being out in the woods on trails. But if you are so stressed by the horse show life or always terrified on the trail, it's ok to decide that that's not for you. Your life will be less stressful! Maybe it's a matter of simply changing the type of horse activity you are involved in, maybe it means changing the type of horse you ride, or maybe it's tougher than that and you need to get out of horses or not own a horse and find a way more fitting to you to be involved in the equine world.

*It's better to know some of the questions than all of the answers.*

—James Thurber,
writer

I have found it frustrating at clinics when I have a question but I can't figure out how to ask it. In my mind, I try to break the question down to a question I can ask and work from there. Many times when I do that, I find I can already answer the smaller questions myself!

*What's important is finding out what works for you.*

—Henry Moore,
sculptor

*O*ver my years of getting back into horses, I have struggled
with pain in my hip area. With daily stretching and regular chiropractic visits and ibuprofen, I have been able to manage the
pain to some degree. However, I have had to come to some conclusions about what kind of horse life I can expect to have.

Part of that has been to realize that when my friends call
and invite me on 4-hour trail rides over somewhat rugged terrain, my body simply can't take it. Halfway through the ride I
am miserable, then my horse becomes miserable. I have had to
admit that I would be content if I spent the rest of my horse life
just tooting around the trails in my own 90-acres of woods. I
keep myself entertained by getting a new horse once in a while!

*Learning when "enough is enough" is the discipline of a lifetime.*

—Gail Godwin,
writer

I think of the phrase "enough is enough" when I see people at clinics who have come to change behavior in their horse that they have simply tolerated long enough. It doesn't matter how that horse got the behavior. When enough becomes enough, it's time to focus on the behavior and what the human is doing to encourage it. If you are lucky enough to have several horses in your lifetime, you would come to find that "enough" comes a lot sooner with each horse.

*Accept the past as the past, without destroying or discarding it.*

—Morne Schwartz

Trying to get back to being balanced and confident in an English saddle, I took lessons and rode around my place on my own A/P saddle with my best riding horse. One day I fell off. We were coming up alongside the barn at the end of a short ride and my reins had a pretty huge loop in them when I asked my mare for a little ride-ending lope up the hill and onto the lawn; at about the time she picked up the lope, something ran into the bushes and she bolted instead. I was totally unprepared and just when I thought I had collected my reins and position enough to get her shut down, she realized King Kong wasn't chasing us and slammed on the brakes. I was still enough out of position that I just came off when her feet stuck into the ground.

I got back on for a few minutes, and in my rides since I made sure to pay more attention, support my horse, and not forget my little tumble. Remembering and learning from the past while moving on doesn't mean constantly recreating or reliving the past.

*Deserve first, then desire.*

—Anonymous

Maybe I want my horse to be better out on the trail or more confident about jumping or more interested and less fearful in working a cow. But if I want this out of my horse, I need to give her what she needs from me to deserve her confidence in what we are attempting to do.

# SEPTEMBER 11

*The world is your playground. Why aren't you playing?*

—Ellie Katz

Those of us who are lucky enough to have horses have the ultimate toy for the playground. I try to remind myself of that when I procrastinate about riding. On 11 September 2001, the day terrorist attacks changed contemporary America, I unglued myself from the television in late afternoon and saddled up. Some people believed that enjoying themselves like that was unsympathetic in light of such a tragedy but it became crystal clear that having horses outside my door is a luxury and while the world as I know it is still intact, I'm going to enjoy those horses. I felt like if any of the people who had lost their lives that morning would have been able to give anyone still alive a piece of advice it would be "do what you love as often as you can because you never know what's going to happen."

*It has often been my mistakes and miscalculations that have taught me the most valuable lessons.*

—from *Considering the Horse*
by Mark Rashid

Many people get hung up on what I think of as "good horse, bad horse" syndrome. The horse is what it is—just because she does or doesn't respond to us in the way we are seeking at a particular time doesn't make the horse "bad." The mistake is in our own communication, not in anything the horse is doing. The horse is simply doing what she thinks is the right thing to do, or if she doesn't understand she is simply doing what she thinks she has to for her own self-preservation. These are great times to figure out how to better communicate with the horse.

*"Are you sure you've ridden a horse before?"*
*"Oh yes."*
*"Then what kind of saddle would you like, with a horn or without?"*
*"I'll take the one without the horn. I doubt I'll run into much traffic."*

—from *The Everything Kids' Joke Book*
by Michael Dahl

This is kind of the approach I take whenever I'm on vacation and go on a trail ride at one of those rent-a-horse stables or when I begin to take lessons. I finally learned that if you say you've ridden before, they give you Old Barn Sour who bolts for the barn at top speed the minute the group is headed in that direction. Or Miss Kick-and-Bite who makes you play dodge-the-weapon when you are saddling her up for your lesson. Now, I just say I haven't ridden much and I get the quiet older horse. The trail horse is just going along a track anyway and in lessons my progress in whatever discipline I am looking to learn will indicate whether I warrant moving up to a more challenging horse or not.

*When a man begins to reason, he ceases to feel.*

—French proverb

When trying maneuvers that are being shown to me at a clinic, I have often found that I am thinking and trying so hard I am not paying enough attention to how things feel with my horse. I get so caught up in the position of my reins or how much bend is in the neck or where my leg is that I'm not feeling when the horse is stepping too shallow behind or when that front leg is just about to leave the ground and so I lose the moment to get what I am hoping to ask the horse for. I guess that's why there's a clinician there to help and to ask "Did you feel that??" when things fall into place.

*One of panic's greatest weapons is its surprise attacks.*
*The best way to combat this weapon is to plan ahead*
*for specific times when you are susceptible to panic.*

—R. Reid Wilson

My mare was almost eight years old before I stopped automatically checking her out on the end of the lead rope before getting on. I may still do that at times if I haven't ridden her for a while or she is acting a little extra frisky or inattentive. The purpose of all that for me is to avoid as much as possible having to deal with things while I'm in the saddle that might make me panic and make things worse. I know I can' t avoid typical horse things all together—like spooking or bolting in fear. But if I can remind the horse that his focus should now be with me and if I can get on confident that I have control of all four feet, then I can certainly decrease the number of instances when my panic button gets hit.

*The perceptive rider allows a mutually inclusive energy to flow between him/herself and the horse, staying in the moment, neither dwelling on the past nor anticipating the future.*

—from *Dressage in the Fourth Dimension*
by Sherry L. Ackerman

I have felt this mutually inclusive energy perhaps a few fleeting times in my quest to improve my horsemanship. These glimpses of "true unity" keep me ever striving to better my riding and to have those moments more often.

*Always smile when you are riding because it changes your intent.*

—James Shaw, Tai Chi instructor,
as quoted on riderswest.com

At a clinic I overheard several people talk about a man who always looked angry when he was riding. And his response when things went a little awry was, in fact, to immediately get grouchy with the horse. Perhaps if that man could consciously smile when he rode, maybe he'd go through a moment or two with a different intent before he got to grouchy, and as a result maybe his horse would react different and then just maybe the man would never make it to the grouchy stage.

*Any type of re-education contains an element of danger and risk of injury to the horse.*

—from *Equus Cabullus*
by Jan May

Having watched many clinicians work to re-educate spoiled horses, I have seen firsthand what the horse (not to mention the handler) has to go through to change undesirable habits. When people criticize some of the horsemen I admire for being too tough on a horse at a clinic, I try to point out that the horse wouldn't have to go through this if the human had cared about and learned better handling in the first place. At least the horse owner is looking for a change. Getting to that change can be tough on the horse but it is usually worth it in the end if the owner is willing to learn and do what it takes to change his or her attitude in order to maintain the horse's new attitude.

*Every time you fall, you learn somethin' new 'bout your horse. You learn what not to do next time.*

—from *Riding Freedom*
by Pam Muñoz Ryan

Yes, you need to be looking to not do again whatever it was that caused you to fall off your horse but not by avoiding things. For example, if your dog comes out of the bushes beside your round pen and your horse jumps and bolts and gets you off, you don't want to simply decide you need to put the dog in the house every time you ride in the round pen. Then you start to avoid things and look to create a "perfect" environment to ride in. Pretty soon that means you can't ride at 2:30 when the school buses start rolling by. Or when it's windy. Suddenly you're like the notorious "bubble boy" on horseback—you need a sterile environment in order to ride.

Expose the horse to some things in a controlled environment, perfect your timing, take some riding lessons and get better balanced, get your horse bending more so you can more quickly shut his engine down, learn more about where that "line" is for your horse so you can get right up to it and keep moving it farther ahead but not cross it—there are lots of things you can do besides create that sterile bubble!

*No man who is occupied in doing a very difficult thing, and doing it well, ever loses his self-respect.*

—George Bernard Shaw,
playwright

Working at becoming more skilled in horse handling and riding is the most difficult task I've ever undertaken. My self-respect kicks in when I remember that I've not only tried hard but have never stopped trying and I have, in fact, come a long way from my first exposure to good horsemanship back in 1991.

*When you give a lesson in meanness to a critter or a*
*person, don't be surprised if they learn their lesson.*

—Will Rogers,
humorist

All those "rogue" horses out there have often simply learned a good lesson. And the word "meanness" can easily be replaced by "disrespect," a lesson we can unwittingly teach our horses on a daily basis.

*There's no perfection, but great satisfaction in trying.*

—Rosalyn Dexter

Perfection actually sounds a bit boring—not that I have any direct experience to speak from!

*That's something people do a lot, mistake dull for gentle.*

—Greg Eliel
at a clinic May 2001

*O*ne place this can really show up is in sacking out. I once was riding my mare in a clinic and the clinician was "flagging" us all, using his flag to help us get soft in taking the hindquarters over, and following with the front quarters. He came up to me with his flag to help me get my horse to move freely and the flag did not phase her. He said something like "First, I've got to get her not dull to the flag." Being an expert horseman, he was able to quickly have her understand when that flag meant to move her feet and when it wasn't intended to mean anything. I saw firsthand that they can distinguish and this has been one of the key moments in my understanding of good horsemanship. Now, when someone tells me, "Oh, the flag won't bother him at all," I know to suspect that the horse is dull to the flag and that I will need to first show the horse that sometimes the flag should hold meaning to him.

I've seen this dull/gentle theory go the other way too—that to make a horse gentle will make it dull. What is referred to as "spirit" usually looks like disrespect to me. A horse can look pretty fired up and moving right out but as long as you have control of the feet and the mind, and some respect going on between the horse and the human I would consider that horse to be gentle—and more what I desire.

*Mistakes are the portals of discovery.*

—Anonymous

I always worried about making the Big Mistake with a horse and "ruining" her. As much as ten years passed before I finally stopped worrying about it so much—even if I do "ruin" a horse, it won't be with malice. The horse ultimately will probably have a better home with me than many other places it could end up. I will always keep working to undo anything I have done "wrong"—and the minute I think I've got something taken care of something else appears, or reappears, anyway!

*A lot of people think they would like to have everything working well, but if it's going to be that much trouble, they decide they don't need it.*

—from *True Unity*
by Tom Dorrance

I am a bit naïve and it took me a while to realize that some people are just satisfied with good enough. It's not until they get desperate—usually the horse starts doing something that scares them—that the outside limit of "enough" gets moved ahead.

*Don't wait for your ship to come in, swim out to it.*

—Anonymous

One way I swim out to my ship when it comes to horses is to get a new horse. A new horse to handle and ride and learn from seems to be a quicker way for me to learn than waiting for things to come up with the horses I already work with.

For instance, I currently have a new colt in the barn. He's a yearling who hasn't been handled much. Although he is a kind, willing horse, things do come hard for him at first and, of course, he exhibits the friskiness that simply comes with being young. Leading him from one place to another requires an awareness that I may have become a bit complacent about with my older horses.

Until this colt arrived on the scene, my Arab filly was the youngster around the barn. Now, leading her, I realize that my attitude about her has become different. For no other apparent reason than the fact that now every day I handle a horse four years younger than she is, my Arab has immediately become older and more mature to me. Walking her from one place to another, I feel that I have a different horse on the end of the lead rope.

You can also accomplish this is by trying something completely new with your horse. Maybe this year instead of trail riding all the time, you might try going to some local horse shows. Your trail rides will seem polished and a piece of cake!

*Teaching others teaches the teacher.*

—from a Dell crossword "Figgerit"

Whenever I try to teach someone about all that I've learned about horsemanship in the past ten years, I invariably think I learned more than my "student." Try it once in a while—young people can be the most challenging. They aren't as willing to intellectualize, they often simply want to get on and ride. Typically kids are pretty flexible and sticky in the saddle so it takes a good teacher to get them revved up about something a little more mentally than physically challenging that they maybe don't think they need.

*Every horse, without exception, will find its way to the skill level of its owner or handler.*

—Frannie Burridge, Owner,
Piper Ridge Farm, Limerick, Maine

This goes back to the "bombproof horse" thing again. The horse who is "bombproof" for one person may well not be as confident in the hands of someone the horse does not feel comfortable with. If the person is a novice and doesn't have much to offer the horse, the horse may not find the support it needs. If the horse is older then it can probably continue to get along pretty well just by drawing on years of experience. But some horses hold it together simply from the confidence it gets from the human.

This can get very evident with horses who are pretty defensive. A friend has a horse that a disreputable dealer would probably advertise as bombproof to ride, but the horse will attack you when you go to get her from her corral. However, if you have a lot of awareness and presence with horses and don't give the mare a chance to attack the first time you approach her, she will never try it with you again. But the novice handler would be in a lot of trouble with this horse. The handler who is skilled and aware can get by great with the mare, the handler who is not skilled could get hurt.

*I have some idea in mind, but the result is always very different from what I really had in mind.*

—Raphael Soyer

Having an idea in mind but having something else happen is better than starting out with no idea at all. The best clinicians that I go to regularly start out with a general plan for the clinic but adapt to whatever comes up. In my own riding, until I get more precise, I am satisfied when I make progress in something even if it wasn't what I set foot in the stirrups to accomplish that day.

————•+•————

*September tries its best to have us forget summer.*

—Bern Williams

Although for those of us in the north, fall means that winter is coming, it's nice that fall is also the best time to ride. This is often the time of year, after having been to several clinics, when I'm ready to abandon the clinic scene and just ride through the woods and see if I can follow through in "real life" with what I've learned in clinics.

*Learn from the turtle. It only makes progress when it sticks its neck out.*

—anonymous from the Internet

$\mathcal{A}$ clinician I've ridden with a couple of times talked to us once about the importance of stretching our comfort zone with our horses. He made it clear that he wasn't suggesting we put ourselves in grave danger or unsafe situations, but it was apparent that many of us were living sheltered horse lives, afraid to let our horses move out or try something that made us a tad uncomfortable and to trust our horses. One way that some of these horsemanship clinics try to stretch riders is by teaching us a little bit about working cows with our horses. I have been in many clinics where riders in dressage saddles are learning and teaching their horses about how to work a cow. Sometimes it ends up no more than teaching the horse not to be afraid of the cows, but everyone is usually beaming with pride in both themselves and their horses by the end!

*A good man is concerned with the welfare of his animals.*

—Proverbs 12:10

I have a theory that all children should be taught to love and respect animals as an integral part of their development into caring adults. Although I have several friends who do not relate to animals at all and have no interest in having pets in the house, most of them simply are not willing to take on the time, expense, or mess that's involved in animal care (and when I can't sit down in my own home with dress clothes on because there's dog hair in every chair, I can relate…). That's ok, that's practicality. It's the people who find animals dispensable that I mistrust. Giving children the sense that animals—frogs, flies, pet cats, whatever—are dispensable is teaching them the first thing about not appreciating life in any form.

*The sooner you treat him like a broke horse, the sooner
he'll act like a broke horse.*

—Harry Whitney,
horseman

The old self-fulfilling prophecy can be very true with horses.
There's a fine line between being cautious and careful about the
stage the horse's education is at and trying to push that stage
forward by treating the horse as if it were already there. If you
continually ride your horse like you are riding on eggs, the
horse will never get comfortable either.

*That is what learning is. You suddenly understand something you've understood all your life, but in a new way.*

—Doris Lessing

I have felt this "new way" of understanding many times after attending many clinics. Even after having heard some concept covered many times before, a new teacher or even the same teacher I've learned from many times says that same old thing in a particular way and it hits the right spot in my brain and clicks.

I suspect some of that happens with the horse as well, it's just a matter of trying enough times to find the right thing that works with that horse to teach it what you are trying to teach it.

*There comes that mysterious meeting in life when*
*someone acknowledges who we are and what we can be,*
*igniting the circuits of our highest potential.*

—Rusty Berkus

Horses often provide that mysterious meeting. It doesn't even have to be someone who is new to horses, sometimes it's just a new horse that makes us realize how much we could actually do with horses.

*Rules which make the most sense to the horse are the ones that are consistent with herd life.*

—from *Influencing the Horse*
by Jim McCall

If you threw a human into the middle of a wild herd and expected us to get along, we would appreciate if the horses could explain the rules of the herd in human terms. And so the horse only logically might be able to better understand the rules of interacting with humans if they are presented within the context of rules it already knows.

*After man has done all he can, it remains for the individual horse to decide how much he is willing to give.*

—from *The Treasury of Horses*
by Walter D. Osborne
and Patricia H. Johnson

Individual horses are so different in what they have to give as well! My gelding, who seems to have a very high level of self-preservation, is able to contribute almost nothing to our relationship. For a long time I found him frustrating and it made me become disinterested in him. Now that I am a little more skilled and have a couple other horses under my belt, I find this gelding more intriguing. For years, I joked that he was probably going to live forever much to my chagrin. Now I worry that he or I won't live long enough for me to ever learn what I need to know to get along better with him.

*When the only tool you own is a hammer, every problem begins to resemble a nail.*

—Abraham Maslow

Working with horses requires many and varied tools. But the tools don't have to be equipment. The best tools are the tools in your mind—if you are going to rely on one tool, the "feel" tool is probably the best one you could focus on. Feel is sort of like riding a bicycle or maybe one of those new Segway personal transportation scooters that Dean Kamen invented. You know you need to move in a certain way, offset your balance, shift your weight, and the vehicle will respond. But you can't explain that exactly to someone else. You just feel it and you feel the moment of response from the vehicle and you act accordingly. And with a horse, this is all so much more rewarding and exciting because there is a living thinking being on the other end.

*If you don't like the response, change your approach.*

—Joe Wolter
at a clinic June 1999

The horse is typically doing what she thinks you asked her to, whether you think you asked that or not. So if you change how you ask, you may get the response you are looking for. This can be especially graphic when asking a reluctant horse to get into a horse trailer. Sometimes it just takes a little change to make things look completely different to the horse. I was working with my Arab filly on trailer loading at one clinic and she got to the point where I could easily drive her into the trailer but was not comfortable there and came right back out. The clinician suggested that as she started to put her hind legs in, I walk in with her. That was all it took, the rest of the session went quite differently.

*It takes years to build trust and seconds to destroy it.*

—anonymous,
from online mail list

Horses are quite forgiving of our innocent mistakes. But if you betray your horse in a way over something that is very meaningful to your horse, you have a long journey ahead of you to prove yourself all over again. However, if you are not pure in your relationship with your horse to begin with, you may never have gained that trust anyway.

*The probability that we may fail in the struggle ought not to deter us from the support of a cause we believe to be just.*

—Abraham Lincoln,
16th U.S. President

As I've mentioned many times, my now-teenaged gelding has been a long, difficult project for me since I bought him as a two year old. The first couple years I had him, I felt I needed to muddle through as best I could trying not to be killed, and attempted to learn how to handle and ride him. I was not very successful, and then I went through a phase of wanting to sell him. No one bit on that one. Then he hung out at a friend's for a couple years while my filly and I lived in the Upper Midwest. When I moved home, the gelding went to a free lease arrangement for a while. Then he came home. And I got another horse and had worked with a few horses in the meantime. And although these other horses helped me become more skilled in good horsemanship, I still made only baby steps of progress with this gelding.

Through all of this, I was asked if perhaps my preferred approach to horsemanship doesn't work for this horse. So far it hasn't, at least not at my level of understanding and ability. But just because it isn't working with him yet and may never work with him within his (or my…) lifetime, I refuse to give up on an approach to horsemanship that focuses on the horse not the human.

*Only the wisest and the stupidest of men never change.*

—Confucius,
Chinese philosopher

Over the years of learning about good horsemanship and respecting my horses and trying to earn their respect, I have spent much time in a round pen doing things like "hooking them on." The end result is interesting and I have often found it a useful way to get my horse a little focused before getting on. In order to hook them on, I would use the halter or a flag to help get them moving out. They would run around and ignore me, ignore me, ignore me, and I would move the flag and keep them going until they seemed to decide that maybe if they paid attention to me they would get to stop the silly circling.

Then a group of things came together—I had listened to a speaker one weekend, read an article a few days later, worked with my sensitive little Arab filly a few days after that—and I began to feel that I no longer wanted to circle horses around round pens. My feelings about all that changed and began to refine—that if my basic desire is for my horse to like being with me, why would I ever chase her away from me with a flag? It certainly doesn't mean I would never use a round pen again, I have a long way to go to understand what is changing in my thinking, and hopefully I can put my refined feelings into practice once I understand them.

*He who is truly wise gains wisdom from another's mishap.*

—Anonymous

Experienced horse people know that one of the key members of your horse's "team" is the group of other horse owners that you trust and respect. These are the people whose mistakes and successes you learn from.

I go to a lot of clinics and in those clinics is typically one clinician instructing many horse and rider combinations. I have heard participants complain about time spent on a particular horse and rider or that they didn't "get their money's worth" if time wasn't spent specifically on them. You miss a lot of learning opportunities if you think that the only time there was anything to learn is when the clinician is working directly with you and/or your horse. Much of my education at clinics comes indirectly, from watching other people and other classes besides the one I am in.

*Freedom is the right to be wrong, not the right to do wrong.*

—John G. Riefenbaker

Good horsemanship promotes the concept of allowing your horse to make decisions. Sometimes those decisions will be wrong, and that's ok. But often it is misinterpreted that in giving your horse respect as a thinking animal, it is ok that the horse walks all over you, tries to rob your pockets looking for treats, and basically runs the show. But good horsemanship is not only being respectful of your horse, it entails teaching your horse to be respectful of you. In order for a horse to be allowed to think something through without fear of retribution if it is wrong, it has to be okay for the horse to be wrong. But that's quite different from it being ok for the horse to "do wrong."

*People think that a horse is stupid when it shies from a flying sheet of paper only to leap in to the path of a moving car, but one must remember that fear, developing at times of outright panic, is a fundamental characteristic of the horse.*

—from *The Spanish Riding School* as quoted in *The Natural Horse* by Jaime Jackson

I am overly cautious when I ride my horses on paved roads. Although I try not to spend any length of time on heavily traveled roads, when a car is coming from behind I tend to ask my horse to wait at a standstill as much off the road as I can until the car has passed.

I'm not worried about the horse shying at a car—in fact that would be preferable since they would most likely jump away from the car into the side of the road and not into traffic. I am more concerned about things on the side of the road causing my horse to jump into traffic—a silent dog that waits until we are right beside him to jump to the end of his rope or children who suddenly spot "a horsie" and thump down the porch stairs and race out to the end of the driveway to get a closer look. So if a horse learns to not be afraid of cars whooshing by, it makes perfect sense to me that they would jump from an unidentified object into the path of a car, which is something they aren't afraid of, with no idea that the car can hurt them badly.

*An eye for an eye only leads to more blindness.*

—from *Cat's Eye*
by Margaret Atwood

J am the first to admit that if a horse bites me, I have difficulty not immediately reacting with a whack. But that whack
really only makes me feel better. Punishment really has no place
in good horsemanship. My responsibility in the relationship
with horses is to become a good enough horsewoman that no
horse that I handle would ever dream of biting me.

*Beware of all enterprises that require new clothes.*

—Henry David Thoreau,
naturalist

When a cowboy first presented "good horsemanship" to those of us in my area, his halter of choice was a rope halter. It didn't take too long before all it took to make people think you were a good horseman and had a certain approach to horses was to hang a rope halter on your horse. Heck, you almost could just hang it in your barn and not even use it, and people would still associate you with the better approach that the clinician was showing us.

Don't be duped by this kind of thing. The person who has spent her entire horse life using spurs for punishment, forcing horses into a physical frame by mechanical means such as martingales, or mindlessly lunging horses for hours, is not suddenly practicing a different kind of horsemanship because she now uses rope halters instead of web halters. This all comes from inside, not from these outward signs.

*When we multiply tiny pieces of time with small increments of daily effort, we too will find we can accomplish magnificent things.*

—Anonymous

J keep getting frustrated by the fact that my gelding and I do not get along. I have had little success riding him. After 11 years together, I thought I at least finally had groundwork down with him until he spooked at something when I was putting him in his stall for dinner one evening and before I even had his halter off he bolted out the door, knocked me on my back, and stepped on my thigh and my chest, breaking one of my ribs. A sure sign that, when push really comes to shove, this horse has little respect for me....

What I do keep coming back to however, is that I have never really spent these consistent, daily small increments of time working with this horse. Over these 11 years, it has been in fits and starts. Some springs, I have gotten the fever to get him in shape for "really riding this year." Off we go to the round pen every day to build him up. That lasts a week to 10 days. Or maybe I'll put him in a clinic and really accomplish something with him. That lasts for the length of the clinic and maybe two weeks after.

I need to really work on this horse consistently and daily and see if I can make any major progress. The turning point may be that of late I have finally come to a point in my own horsemanship skills that I find the horse more fascinating than frustrating.

*What would you attempt to do if you knew you could not fail?*

—Anonymous

J have been on a search lately to find something to do with horses, some sort of mini-adventure or something new. One of the things I have always thought about doing is working with young kids and their horses in some way or another. Ultimately, I decided that this horse stuff is my private thing that I do to stay emotionally balanced and I am not willing to share my horse day with people on a regular basis. Then I thought maybe I could buy horses that are selling cheaply, the kind people are looking to get rid of for whatever reason, and "recondition" them to be kid-safe, and sell horses based on that premise, giving a short series of lessons with each horse as it is sold. But putting the numbers together, I just couldn't see how you could make it work financially.

So I still haven't figured out what I would attempt to do if I knew it couldn't fail, but the search is kind of fun!

*To find new things, take the path you took yesterday.*

—John Burroughs,
naturalist

$\mathcal{E}$very time you do something with your horse that you did the last time you worked with him, you will find that there is something new to work on. The nice thing about horses is that if you learn to appreciate that they are living, thinking creatures and don't get tricked with all the gimmicks out there into trying to make them into mechanical, non-thinking machines, you will have an ever-changing experience on your hands and you will certainly never be bored.

*If nothing changes, nothing changes.*

—seen on a
bumper sticker

If your horse is exhibiting behavior that you find undesireable and you don't change anything you are doing, your horse's behavior won't change either.

*Opportunity is missed by most people because it is dressed in overalls and looks like work.*

—Thomas Edison,
inventor

I have heard people at clinics on good horsemanship claim they have done what the clinician is doing all their lives and that it is so nice to see someone getting their ideas out to the public. But I know their horses and know that is not the case. Other people have gone to one clinic and tell me that they and their horses now have a complete understanding and have everything the clinician taught them down perfectly. It's probably that I am a little slow, but I have been to literally dozens of clinics and I still have a long way to go. Or maybe these people work at it lots harder than I do, but I still know that "this stuff" is not had in one clinic. If you get hooked on this idea of good horsemanship, get your overalls on!

*Happiness hides in life's small details. If you're not looking, it becomes invisible.*

—Dr. Joyce Brothers

One of the small things I have come to thoroughly enjoy with what I have learned about the way I'd like to interact with my horses is that small gesture of offering their head when I go to put their halters on. This tiny piece of giving, of cooperation now makes me smile every time. I never not notice it.

*Nobody cares if you can't dance well. Just get up and dance.*

—Dave Barry

The participants in a class at a clinic often feel self-conscious being watched by the spectators around the ring. It can feel like a horse show where you are judged rather than a clinic where you are there to learn about things you don't know or aren't too polished in. But having been a spectator many times as well, I know that even though the participants may think that everyone is watching every move they make, they aren't. Spectators are trying to keep tabs on everyone—even when the clinician singles out one rider to work with and the focus is on him or her, the spectators are mostly thankful they are sitting on the sidelines and not in the hot seat!

*Those who master others have force. Those who master themselves have strength.*

—Lao-tzu,
Chinese philosopher

Working with horses seems to be around 90% working on yourself and your attitude and approach and ability and 10% working on the horse.

*Imagination is more important than knowledge.*

—Albert Einstein,
physicist

Without being able to imagine something, we cannot have much of an impact on it. Stretch your imagination about what you can accomplish with your horse. That may mean no more than being able to go to the end of the driveway and pick up the mail or as much as jumping over a three-jump line. Go out of the box and do things you didn't imagine doing. Maybe you are into showing in Western Pleasure—stretch yourself in the off-season and take some dressage lessons. If you tend toward the hunter-jumper circuit, go find a place to work a few cows. You will really need to stretch your imagination to find the ways that these activities that are unrelated to what you do most of the time have anything to teach you about your chosen equestrian activity.

*If you shut your door to all errors, truth will be
shut out.*

—Rabindranath Tagore,
writer

We all seem to be able to intellectually understand that we can learn from our own mistakes and the mistakes of others. But we still often try to avoid mistakes at the expense of stretching and learning, and we beat ourselves up when we do make them. Maybe every time we make a "mistake" working with our horses we should make it a habit to stop if we can and reflect a couple minutes on what that mistake can teach us. If it's not convenient to do that at that moment, tuck it away and be sure to reflect on it later. Sometimes it helps to talk it out with a sympathetic friend.

*To tell the truth, I could work one flower forever.*

—Nell Blaine

*S*ome people have the focus to work with one horse for years, perfecting their technique and relationship with that one horse. I seem to need to work with several horses to advance my abilities. My problem is that I am not skilled enough to take in other people's horses and can't afford to keep buying them and owning them! Right now, my approach is to buy them with the intention of selling them after I've been able to feel that we both have made some progress in some area.

———•———

*A lot of people approach risk as if it's the enemy when it's really fortune's accomplice.*

—Sting in *A Man's Journey to Simple Abundance*

Risk is a funny thing, it's very different for everyone. Some people feel that risk is riding your horse when the wind is blowing. Other people feel that risk is galloping through a field. Others feel that risk is getting on a horse at all. The key to feeling positive about risk is to learn what your risk tolerance is and stretch ever so slightly and ever so slowly beyond it. That's where progress happens.

*The challenged life may be the best therapist.*

—Gail Sheehy

$S$tepping outside your comfort zone once in a while can be the most exhilarating experience. If you can do that enough times and have it work out okay, the times when it doesn't work out become less discouraging.

*In the mind of the beginner, all things are possible.*
*But in the mind of the expert, only a few.*

—D. T. Suzuki

When I go to clinics and watch people new learning about groundwork, I can go right back to when I first was exposed to good horsemanship as well. I can feel the lead rope so awkward in my hands, I can remember thinking I "got it" when I asked the horse to step over behind, rock back, bring it's front end across, and go in the other direction—until I really did get it, and realized that all that time the horse had never really stepped over or never really got soft. After all these years, I always still feel like a beginner, which is a nice place to be in for me.

*You can pull him harder and get it faster, but I want him to search for it. I just do less, and wait longer. Waiting seems slower, but by far it's the short cut in the long run.*

—Bryan Neubert,
clinic, Arizona 2000

This waiting thing is a hard one for most of us humans. We have such a tendency to be in a big hurry to get something accomplished. The horse doesn't care how long it takes or even if you ever accomplish it for that matter. Most are just going along with the deal. Think about how forgiving an animal that must be!

*The mediocre teacher tells.*
*The good teacher explains.*
*The superior teacher demonstrates.*
*The great teacher inspires.*

—William A. Ward

The legendary horseman Tom Dorrance is probably the perfect example of the great teacher. I have only met him once so I don't know, but I suspect he went through the three earlier stages that are mentioned in this quote. Now in his nineties, Dorrance is no longer out doing clinics or teaching people with their horses, but he is certainly an inspiration to be a better horseman or horsewoman to all who run across his teachings through his book, *True Unity*, a couple of videos, and stories from those who know him well.

---

*Patience and time do more than strength or passion.*

—Jean La Fontaine,
poet

$S$trength and passion are certainly helpful when working with horses. Without passion, it would be difficult to do the hard work that it takes to just keep a horse, let alone work with it. And it does take some strength, maybe just hold a flag for any length of time, lift a heavy saddle gently upon a horse's back, and countless other ways.

But if you could only pick two things, definitely pick patience and time. Those are the things that would get you the farthest. With my three horses who are now over five and I have had since they were yearlings or younger, I have found it interesting how just time (i.e., age and experience) has helped change some things with them.

*How we think shows through in how we act. Attitudes are mirrors of the mind. They reflect thinking.*

—David Joseph Schwartz

Horses are quickly able to pick up on a person's attitude. Some people try to fake it and pretend they are interested in good horsemanship no matter how long it takes. And they probably are, but often only if it can quickly accomplish what they want to accomplish with the horse! Many people are not willing to take the time it might take to get something done through good horsemanship and not a gimmick or other shortcut. The horse knows whether you are sincere in your attitude or not, it's all they've got to go on.

*I want to stay as close to the edge as I can without going over. Out on the edge, you can see all kinds of things you can't see from the center.*

—from *Player Piano*
by Kurt Vonnegut, Jr.

Once again, we get back to the idea of pushing your and your horse's comfort zone. When I go on a trail ride with my eight-year-old mare, I let her settle in for a while and then I push her and my comfort zone. I may let the rest of the group get out of sight; she definitely gets upset and we spend some time doing serpentines and circling and moving her hind over, rocking back, coming across with the front. By the time I've got her concentrating on moving her feet quite a bit, she calms down. She doesn't forget about the group ahead, but she does consider them quite a bit less important. It's her prerogative to get concerned about the rest of the group—her feelings are her feelings. I just try to set it up for her to change her feelings and become okay with just the two of us being alone.

Although I am not a good enough horsewoman yet for this to stick permanently, I do get a thrill out of watching it all shape up. However, always keep right on the edge of your and your horse's comfort zone, don't push too far beyond it to the point of getting into trouble—not only is that not safe, but you can actually end up accomplishing the opposite of what you really want when the horse realizes that being alone with you really isn't the safe place you claim it is!

*I don't want to be a source of aggravation*
*[to my horse ], I want to be a source of comfort.*

—Mark Rashid,
The Horse Gathering 2001

There are some who would consider "being a source of comfort" to your horse being "soft." Although there are certainly occasions when it is important to firm up with a horse, that tough-guy approach is unfortunate because it clearly doesn't make the horse feel very good and it can't make the human feel very good either.

*Stress is an ignorant state. It believes that everything
is an emergency.*

—from *Wild Mind*
by Natalie Goldberg

We all see this happen in clinics—some riders feel that every little flinch the horse makes is an emergency and an impending tragedy! Or we have friends we ride with who are so stressed that they are frightened by their horse's every move. Our horses probably feel the same when they are stressed—in that state of being, everything that occurs is something to treat as an emergency. This certainly creates a little bit of the classic vicious circle—if you are super stressed, your horse is super stressed, and therefore your stress level continues or increases because your horse's stressed-out actions are stressful to you! Probably the only two ways to combat this are to do things to help your own stress level decrease and find a horse whose natural stress level is pretty low. That kind of been-there-done-that horse may allow the rider to gain enough confidence to maintain a lower stress level on a horse who has the potential for a bit higher stress level, thus breaking the cycle.

*I believe in an open mind, but not so open that your brains fall out.*

—Arthur Hays Sulzberger

Trying to be open minded while being firmly entrenched in the things you have definitely come to believe is a tough line to walk. But being so open minded to everything that comes down the pike is also not very helpful. One needs to have a solid line to walk in order to veer off it when something interesting comes along.

*Writing a novel is like driving at night. You can only see as far as your headlights let you, but you can make the whole trip that way.*

—E. L. Doctorow

You can approach attaining good horsemanship this way too. You may only be able to see what's right ahead of you but as soon as you take care of that, the next section of the road becomes visible.

*There are a million things in music I know nothing about. I just want to narrow down that number.*

—Andre Previn

I begin to realize how far away I am from being a good horsewoman when I try to help someone else. Oh, I may be able to help them get through something they are working on, yet I probably have the same issue with at least one of my horses. This ends up making me one of those mediocre teachers who can explain but it's hard to be a teacher-by-example when you are unable to get over the same hump within your own horse-manship. It still is all worth doing though, because in explaining to others I tend to advance my own thinking while still being able to help them at least somewhat.

*Common sense tells us that success makes people optimistic. But…the arrow goes in the opposite direction as well. Optimistic people become successes.*

—Martin E. P. Seligman, PhD

I maintain what I refer to as practical optimism. There is no point in false optimism—if you aren't optimistic, faking it is going to make you feel worse than being negative. I don't know whether it is age or experience, but I have started to quite unconsciously avoid people who are in a constant negative state of mind. I find it just brings me down; life's too short for that! I believe that anyone can do whatever it is they choose to do as long as they are practical about their choices.

*Success or failure in business is caused more by mental attitude than mental capacities.*

—Walter Dill Scott,
executive

This continues on the theme of optimism and belief in what you can do. You don't need to be a genius to be successful at a business venture or a horse project. You need to believe you can succeed and work from that frame of mind. This attitude will allow you to recognize when you need help, when you need to change your approach, when you need to work on some other aspect of the project, which continues the chain of success.

*If you start with something false, you're always covering your tracks.*

—Paul Simon

*O*ne thing I have found with working toward good horse-manship is that you really do have to believe in this way of being throughout your entire body and mind. Otherwise, you are deceiving everyone and you spend a lot of time covering your tracks, hiding the things that you do when no one is looking.

*A teacher enlarges people in all sorts of ways besides just his subject matter.*

—from *Crossing to Safety*
by Wallace Stegner

When you teach your horse things like the "soft feel" you are teaching the horse not just the simple action of bending at the poll when you pick up on the reins, you are teaching her a way of life—to yield, not resist.

*I have three phobias which, could I mute them, would make my life as slick as a sonnet, but as dull as ditch water.*

—Tallulah Bankhead

I've heard people apologize for their horse's undesireable behaviors and say "well, she's still a work in progress." What I have come to understand about those of us who dig up every spare penny to go to clinics each year is that we like the "work in progress" part of having horses. We aren't looking for bombproof horses or some sort of endpoint, we are looking to work with horses to help them have a better life and teach us something about horsemanship in the process. And we don't mind if the process never ends. And although the expert horsemen talk about making a finished horse, I believe even they are probably always working on something with that horse, and they are definitely working with fresh horses all the time to keep working on the process—their idea of a finished horse always keeps getting moved ahead.

*If a child can't learn the way we teach, maybe we should teach the way they learn.*

—Ignacio "Nacho" Estrada

The concept of considering learning style is what I see as somewhat the foundation of good horsemanship. Historically, humans have always expected horses to fit into their program; however the human saw fit to "break" the horse to a saddle, for instance, is the way the horse was expected to deal with it. In this new trend toward being mindful of how the horse perceives all of these new things we want her to do, we can end up with a horse who is more content and not defensive about all the things that are being thrown at her that she cannot understand and therefore finds threatening based on her own need for self-preservation. Teaching a horse in a manner that takes into consideration how the horse learns only makes good sense.

*A piece of sculpture or a painting is never a finished work. Simultaneously, it answers a question which has been asked, and asks a new question.*

—Robert Engman

New questions are always coming up in my day-to-day interactions with horses. In some ways this is supremely frustrating, in other ways it is exactly what keeps my interest in horses fresh and intriguing.

*A lot of people are teaching their horse something that they don't have a clue they are teaching their horse.*

—Harry Whitney
at The Horse Gathering 2001

J cannot count the times I have heard numerous clinicians remind their students that with every interaction you have with your horses, you are teaching them something whether you know it or not, whether you want the horse to be learning that thing or not. Even walking into the paddock is an education for the horse in human/horse relations.

*People will forget what you said. People will forget what you did. But they won't forget the way you made them feel.*

—Anonymous

In order to understand more fully what I believe is the best way to work with horses, I watch every clinician whose path I can run across. Recently I was at a demonstration by a successful clinician. He was doing some groundwork with the horse in preparation for loading the horse into a horse trailer. In doing the groundwork, he used a flag to extend his reach and offer more impact. All this fits in with anything I have learned and come to respect—that loading a horse in a trailer is often, at least at first, not about the trailer, but about moving and directing the horse's feet. That a flag can be a useful tool if used appropriately.

The trouble with the approach I was seeing that day is that the clinician described his use of the flag as for "annoying" the horse. Imagine the horse's feelings when this man was "annoying" her. He could have whacked her on the butt with that flag once to get her going and I bet she would forget that whack, but it will take a lot of makeup time for her to forget that this man spent his time annoying her.

*She's entitled to her thoughts.*

—Ray Hunt about
a mare he was riding

It amazes me that people would think that a living, thinking, breathing animal would not be entitled to its thoughts. That doesn't mean we need to let our horses act on thoughts that will get us both in trouble. But it certainly can mean that we can take into consideration their concerns about a particular situation and try to help them be more comfortable with what is going on. Being aware of what thoughts your horse might be having is the beginning.

*Do not be awestruck by other people and try to copy them. Nobody can be you as efficiently as you can.*

—Norman Vincent Peale

After more than ten years of learning about good horsemanship, I have finally begun to develop my own way of going about things. These are not always the best ways and I can change and adapt when I find a better approach. But I feel I am finally just beginning to see a framework of my own approach with my own horses upon which I can build. And being me is all I can be—I can never be one of the great clinicians I have been privileged to study with or one of the great riders that I admire but I certainly can work that aspiration into my own development as a horsewoman.

*Learn the rules so you know how to break them properly.*

—attributed to the Dalai Lama

Without a frame to work within, you never know if you are veering off into territory you'd rather not be. Many riding teachers, especially in jumping, talk about "riding a line." That imaginary line can tell you whether you are on track or not, whether you need to adjust or remain just as you are.

*Don't put on the pressure. Just ask a little and try to keep what you've got.*

—jumping instructor,
name unknown

$\mathcal{J}$ find this quote difficult to understand in theory, but when I watched a jumping clinic and heard this instructor say this to a couple of upper level riders, it made a lot of sense. The riders' horses clearly had the ability to be very focused but they kept getting very wound up. The instructor was trying to get these riders to push the envelope slowly with their horses so that they could make progress but not lose the horse mentally. So if your horse is going trotting along smoothly and slowly and you want to rev things up a notch, don't pressure her into a fast trot. Wind things up one or two notches at a time—keep the nice trot you have and ask for just a little more. Then keep that while asking for just a notch more. Until what you have is what you want without ever having put so much pressure on the horse she falls apart.

*When you are content to simply be yourself and don't compare or compete, everybody will respect you.*

—Lao-tzu,
Chinese philosopher

In the horse world, it is hard not to compare and/or compete at least some of the time, especially for those whose horse world revolves around competitive events—the very essence is to compete! Being involved in attempting to learn a unique approach to horsemanship, I have also found it difficult not to compare. Sometimes this is the only way to learn and think through your own approach.

If competing and comparing is hard to avoid, perhaps the best way to deal with it is to keep it positive. I have had to find ways to see what other people are doing and find the positive in it while cheerfully rejecting it myself—like using treats for things I know I can accomplish just by learning good horsemanship. Or turning to something I find to be a gimmick when, again, simple good horsemanship would accomplish the same thing with a more thorough understanding on the part of both horse and human.

Compare, compete, and stay positive. It's hard but it's worth it.

*The best way to have a good idea is to have lots of ideas.*

—Linus Pauling,
chemist

Photographers know that the only way to get exactly the shot they are looking for is to shoot lots of film—there will be more of a chance of getting the one picture that doesn't have someone walking by in the background or a telephone pole sticking out of the horse's head or the rider with his eyes shut. I hope that's not the way it is with horses—that to learn to create a really great riding horse you need to go through lots of horses! Although as I continue to add to my collection, I begin to think that's how I approach it.

*Many people consider loading a horse into a trailer*
*as something akin to open heart surgery.*

—from *The Faraway Horses*
by Buck Brannaman

The horse trailer can be a test of all you are as a horse person!
It encompasses every one of the key skills of good horseman-
ship—patience, timing, understanding, trust, some empathy.
Allowing the horse to be a horse.

But you will get nowhere with a horse trailer if you think
loading a horse into one has much to do with the trailer itself.
Of course, the horse needs to be given an opportunity to sniff it
and explore the trailer at hand. Yet the way to get a horse into a
trailer is to get everything done before the trailer ever comes
into the picture. Get your horse thoroughly halter broke so he
respects you on the end of a lead rope, moves his feet where and
when you ask him to. Gain your horse's trust—be completely
consistent so he knows that something means the same thing
every time, that you aren't going to lose your temper with him
and make him feel he has to be defensive, and don't get him into
sticky situations all the time through ignorance or hard headed-
ness. Learn how to communicate with a horse on the horse's
terms, do some of the adjusting yourself don't expect your horse
to do all the adjusting.

Get these things down and you have trailer loading down
before you even get the door open!

*When we blindly adopt a religion, a political system, a literary dogma, we become automatons. We cease to grow.*

—Anais Nin
in *The Diaries of Anais Nin*

J was sitting in a large crowd of people watching a great horseman work with his horse and listening to what he had to say. He described something he was doing as "holding great meaning to the horse" and I burst out to one of my spectating companions "how could he possibly know that for sure?" I hadn't meant to say it out loud and got a couple pretty disgusted looks from a couple people in front of me!

Now, if anyone could know whether something held great meaning to a horse or not, I believed this man could just by his incredible sensitivity to horses. Nonetheless I think as much as we try to understand horses, I'm not sure we will ever know anything about how they think or feel for certain. I guess I don't want to accept everything without questioning even if it is from someone for whom I have the utmost respect and admiration.

*With conditioned response, you're just conditioning bits and parts. When you deal with the mind, it lasts forever.*

—Randy Lowell,
horseman

The problem I find with the idea that dealing with the mind lasting forever is that you need to possess the ability to deal with the mind in a way that will have lasting effect. If the horse does not believe you, does not understand you, or somehow cannot grasp your meaning, it will not last. For instance, I believe I have a great relationship with my mare. She clearly respects me more than she does other people, who she tries to boss around if they give her even an inch. However, despite her apparent respect for me and seeming enjoyment being with me, she still falls apart heading out on the trails on our property having little fits about getting back to the barn or her herd-mates. No matter how good I think things are with her and I, it is clearly only good as long as her herdmates, who really make her feel comfortable, are within range. I have not gotten to her mind enough to give her the support she needs so that she can get that support from me and not the other horses back at the barn.

*No one can teach riding as well as a horse.*

—C.S. Lewis,
writer

Ride, ride, ride is the best way to become a better rider. If you can only ride one horse, well ride that one as much as possible. But if you can ride several, that is an even better way to learn.

*It's not hard to make a decision when you know what your values are.*

—anonymous

*O*nce I became more certain in my understanding of the fundamental way I would like to exist around and interact with my horses, it became easy to make decisions about tack and other equipment and methods and whether they fit my equine values or not.

*Work joyfully and peacefully, knowing that right thoughts and right efforts inevitably bring about right results.*

—James Allen

A lot about "intent" is said in the clinics I attend. If your intentions are not pure, you will never get anywhere even though you will perhaps think you are. But with "right thoughts and right efforts" a lot is possible and will come together almost despite you.

A concrete example of this is how a horse can distinguish between a flag waved at them with energy suggesting that they move and a flag waved at them in anger at something they've done or haven't done. I've learned a lot about being angry at a horse in the years that I've owned my gelding. Get angry with a horse and unless he has one of those relentlessly giving natures, he is usually quite happy to show you what a thousand pound animal looks like being defensive and angry. Believe me, those kicks in your direction or rears and bucks while you are on their backs are no fun. If I could just purify my intent with this horse—that is, truly want to cooperate with him not just talk the talk—I would probably find some big differences.

*Patience: n. A minor form of despair, disguised as a virtue.*

—Ambrose Bierce
in *The Devil's Dictionary*

Ha, ha! Although Bierce has hit on something we can relate to, patience really is a virtue. Impatience has ruined a lot in the horse world from ruining horses when they are young to being so intent on a horse learning something that we mistake forcing her for teaching her. Patience is certainly a difficult thing to learn or maintain but can be the most important trait when dealing with horses.

*Turning on a light does not eliminate fear of the dark,*
*it only eliminates the dark.*

—Paul Bishop
in "Break on Through"
in *Guide to Writing Fiction Today* Winter 2000

Gimmicks and miracle cures for horse problems appear to eliminate the problem, but they don't eliminate the *reason* for the problem you are having—which means without the gimmick the problem is still there. They don't rely on *how* they are used but claim to solve things just *because* they are used. I guess if you don't want to take the time and effort to help the horse solve the underlying issue that is causing the thing that is giving you a problem, then these quick fixes are useful. They certainly make some people wealthy! Unfortunately some problems, like cribbing, tend to not be able to be solved; the key there, of course, is to not let the problem crop up in the first place.

———•—•———

*There is a way of relating that acknowledges the child's*
*equal worth as a human but still makes clear the*
*authority of the parents in the family.*

—Roberta Gilbert
in *Connecting with Our Children*

I constantly run into concepts about children that could apply to horses. My goal is to make sure my horses know that they are in no way less of a being than I am. Our relationship, however, needs a leader and that would be me.

*The art of being wise is the art of knowing what to overlook.*

—William James,
psychologist

The best clinicians are masters at knowing what to overlook. They could be out there nitpicking every little thing their students do but that would really help no one—there wouldn't be enough time for more than two or three students in a clinic and the student would only get frustrated, not encouraged. Instead, they know what the key things are to mention to each student that are fundamentals and will help that student with the many other things in their horsemanship.

*Anything that is forced or misunderstood can never be
beautiful.*

—Xenophon,
Greek historian

The prime example of this, of course, is the severe frame that
horses are sometimes forced into with martingales and tie-downs
to create a look. Sometimes the forced look doesn't even require
a mechanical means to hold it there, the horses have been so
fried by having been "trained on" that they are held in a peculiar
way of going by sheer mental pressure. These are live animals,
not plastic model horses.

*He is able who thinks he is able.*

—Buddha

I don't know if I always believe this. Just because I think I am able to ride a certain way, does not mean I am capable of the focus and effort it would take for me to get there. However, I definitely believe the opposite—if you think you are unable to accomplish something, you will most likely be unable to accomplish it.

*If you don't like something, change it. If you can't change it, change your attitude. Don't complain.*

—Maya Angelou,
writer

$\mathcal{J}$ don't think Angelou meant that you should change your attitude about what you don't like and decide to like it. But the idea of not complaining is one a lot of us could take to heart! I get caught up in it just like everyone else, and occasionally have to step back and remind myself that I do not want to spend my life complaining about things, I would rather spend my time involved in things that I don't need to complain about or that I am trying to have an influence on so that the things I would like to complain about can be made different.

*The secret to happiness is to make others believe they are
the cause of it.*

—Al Batt
in *National Enquirer* as
quoted in *Reader's Digest*

This kind of reminds me of when you can set things up to
make something the horse's idea. If they think they are the cause
of pressure and release themselves from it, they can also think
they are the solution. Then maybe they will always look for the
solution and not get caught up in the pressure to begin with.

*We don't need to have disposable horses, we need to
adjust.*

—Peggy Cummings
at The Horse Gathering 2001

Don't expect the horse to do all the adjusting. You may think
a horse isn't working out for you, but if you work hard enough
to figure out why, you may find that with some adjustments on
your part you have a great horse under you.

*If what you are doing doesn't work, stop doing it.*

—Ferdinand F. Fournies, author
of *Coaching for Improved Work Performance*

This theme keeps coming up, but it is amazing how we get stuck in a certain way of thinking we have to work with a horse hoping that eventually he will get it. Try something else. We all, including horses, learn in different ways and presenting something to the horse in a different way may be just what he needs.

*It is not as much a matter of tennis as it is of mental fitness.*

—Juan Carlos Ferrero,
tennis player

Riding, like tennis, is a thing that can be learned. Mental fitness is what allows us to tackle anything that comes along, to think through the problem using mental skills we can apply to anything.

*It's difficult to injure a relaxed muscle, it's easy to injure a tight one.*

—Dr. Deb Bennett,
The Horse Gathering 2001

Many of my horseriding friends who have not been involved in the approach to horsemanship that I have seem to spend a lot of time on the physical horse—wrapping, blanketing, worrying about lameness issues. I began to question my lack of focus on these things. I asked a clinician about this and our conclusion was that a horse whose foundation is in mental soundness will be much more inclined to stay physically sound. When horses operate from a tense place, they are much more likely to injure themselves. When they are relaxed think about where their feet are, and not just blindly stumble through the ride, they are subject to much less possible injury.

*There are two things over which you have complete dominion, authority, and control—your mind and your mouth.*

—Molefi Keto Asante

There are some things you simply can't blame on anyone else. If you say something, you said it, no one forced you. And what goes on in your mind is for you alone to control. So, think good thoughts and speak accordingly!

*There are two kinds of people who never amount to much: those who cannot do what they are told and those who can do nothing else.*

—Cyrus H. K. Curtis

When working with horses, especially young ones, it is very helpful to be the kind of person who can think creatively and is not afraid to try things. In some clinics I've attended, there are people who really want to be told what to do every step of the way. Sometimes that just comes from inexperience. One of the best clinicians I know has a way of encouraging people to think things through—he acts like he is not paying attention to something going on with a person and his horse, but this clinician sees everything. Although I've never heard him say so, it appears that at some point he is trying to get his students to stop relying on him for every single solution and to work through some of their problems, learning to also rely on their own abilities and instincts, as well as their horse to help teach them how to approach something. It is a great technique.

*Like it or not, you are the horse's primary trainer.*

—Becky Sweeney
in "Homework" in
*The Horse's Maine* January 2002

This is one of the key concepts to being a good horseman or horsewoman. People who want to get a horse and have a trainer teach the horse everything he needs to know, then hand the horse back to the new owner with all the buttons in place should probably just get a motorcycle. Not only are you, the horse's caretaker, responsible for your horse's education, but that education is going on every minute you are with the horse.

———•••———

*Check your own attitude before trying to work on anyone else's.*

—Alex Hiam
in *Making Horses Drink*

Whenever I think that someone else's attitude is too negative or too judgmental or too this or too that, I try to remember to take a close look at my own attitude. Maybe it's just me that needs a fine tuning. Chances are when I get my attitude in shape, I won't really care about other people's attitudes!

*Horses have triple PhDs in spatial relationship.*
*We are at about kindergarten level.*

—Randy Lowell,
horseman

Horses in a group are mostly very respectful of each other. My mare knows that it just is not okay to get too close to her gelding friend when he is eating his hay. If they run through the corral gate, they step back ever so slightly to let the boss go through first. They are very aware of the space around them. The more I learned about respecting a horse's space and teaching my horses to respect mine, the more peaceful our interactions became.

*Wisdom begins in wonder.*

—Socrates,
philosopher

$\mathcal{I}$ have not found any lack of wonderment in my life since I reintroduced myself to the horse world! I don't know how much wiser I have become—perhaps not much since I've just acquired my fourth horse—but I certainly am fascinated on a daily basis.

*...[w]e are all free to choose our attitude.*

—Peter Koestenbaum
in *Fast Company* magazine

No one forces our attitude on us, it is strictly our own. It is very difficult to maintain an attitude that you can feel good about, especially since it's so easy to get caught up in everyone else's attitudes. This doesn't mean that one has to go around having a Pollyanna approach to everything, and always gushing with happiness. That is often disingenuous anyway. But trying to look at things from a positive aspect instead of always looking for the negative can be a very uplifting feeling.

*Being truthful, when you know it will cost you, is the true test of honesty.*

—Dave Weinbaum

A friend once went to an ethics seminar in relation to a volunteer service she was doing. She found the speaker to be very inspirational and said that one of the most thought-provoking comments the speaker made was that in order to practice good ethics, one must be honest in the little things as well as the big things. As I usually do, I immediately connected this to the horse stuff I have been involved in all these years.

Pure honesty is perhaps the best trait a person can have no matter what you are involved in. It always works out better in the long run. And it's the least that your horse should be able to expect from you.

*A true leader is a supporting thing, not a dominating thing.*

—Randy Lowell,
seminar, Northeast Horseman's Trade Show

Leadership is a very misunderstood thing, and I think Randy's quote clearly points out that leadership should have a positive connotation, not a negative one. Employees in business often think of the leaders of the company they work for as domineering people with an elevated sense of self-importance. And while sometimes this is true, it doesn't mean that that is what a good leader should be.

Learn how to be a good leader to your horse and it will be the best thing you could do to improve your relationship.

*I'm telling you, you're greenhousing these horses.*

—Rodney Jenkins,
from video "Three Masters"

$\mathcal{I}$ like this concept "greenhousing." Probably many people have tasted tomatoes direct from the garden; these tomatoes don't always look nice, they can be misshapen and have some dirt on them, but they are sweet and delicious. In the middle of winter, when those of us in the north are starting to crave fresh produce, we are tempted by those red, red tomatoes in the grocery stores, that are grown under optimum conditions, are perfectly and uniformly shaped, and typically taste very bland.

Horses that are kept in artificial environments and are blanketed and kept inside all the time for the benefit of the rider's use or even those that are simply confined by lots of equipment and mental confinement from a rider who spends more time on the physical horse than the mental horse have a look about them that seems like what could be called a "greenhouse" look. They look nice, they are often beautifully groomed and physically fit, but they have either a faraway look or have developed some nasty habits. Horses that are not "greenhoused" but are able to lead a more natural life and life mostly outdoors and are ridden in a way that allows them to use their mind and are not forced to do things in a way that isn't suitable to them seem to show a lot more interest in life and things around them.

*What is the most difficult thing in the equation?*
*Making it simple.*

—George Morris,
from video "Three Masters"

Ah, how we humans try to complicate things! Equipment, stabling, moving horses around, blanketing, supplements. Good horsemanship is quite simple and needs no gimmicks or equipment of any kind. Throw in a basic shelter, quality feed, plenty of water, and there you have the most important parts of horse care.

*If you quit on a good note, they're liable to be as good or better the next day. If you quit on a bad note, they're liable to be as bad or worse the next day.*

—Bryan Neubert,
horseman

This is something that makes good sense. Don't let your horse—or you!—soak on a bad experience by ending your session that way. It's like that old saying that if you fall off a horse it's important to get right back in the saddle. If you aren't hurt, that really is true because if you fall off and wait til next time you will spend that whole time associating riding with falling off. If you get back on, even if it's just for a couple minutes or while someone leads you around, it will give you both a better thing to soak on until your next riding session. The same if you are working on teaching your horse something or taking a ride on a young colt. End the session when things are pleasant for the both of you.

*The mere imparting of information is without
education. Above all things, the effort must result in
man thinking and doing for himself.*

—Carter G. Woodson

It is key, in attending all these clinics and learning things
from reading books and magazines, that ultimately you need to
do the things yourself to really learn. You need to think things
through on your own. When I got back into horses with the
purchase of my gelding, he was at other people's farms for the
first three years. At the last place he was at, I acquired a young
filly and brought them both to my newly purchased farm. It was
not until then that I really felt like I could learn a lot about these
animals—they were mine to care for day-in and day-out and I
learned more in a week than I had in three years.

*The best thing for the inside of a horse is the outside of the barn.*

—Gail Ivey,
horsewoman

There is always a time and a place for putting a horse in a stall and it's important to have a stall available for a sick horse or if the fence breaks or whatever. But for the most part, horses are most comfortable when they are allowed to roam and act like horses.

*What's best for the animals at the end of the day, just like humans, is that they have some purpose.*

—Russell Crowe,
actor, ranch owner

I've tried to concoct things for my horses to do. We bought a cabin at the other end of our property and the first year we owned it, my mare and I would take a ride to it and check on the cabin a couple times a week. I occasionally get the mail with her, even though the driveway is pretty short... Just having something to do with the horses makes it more enticing to go out in the cold or heat or rain and ride.

*We must embrace both joy and pain, embrace gently
without attachment.*

—Philip Simmons,
*Learning to Fall*

I had a great ride on my mare the other day riding out from
the farm to a place we'd never been before. I described it to
someone as the best ride I've had on her in the entire six years
she's been under saddle—she was very forward, no barn sourness, she tried a couple new things with what I consider an
appropriate balance of trepidation but willingness, she seemed
interested in the surroundings, she was very in tune with me. I
would go out on a limb and say I think she may even have
enjoyed the ride.

That was a great ride. But the rides that aren't so great—the
ones where my mare constantly tests me, where she seems to
need to be encouraged almost every step of the way, where she
fusses at stream crossings, I enjoy too.

Life is what it is, and encompasses the things that are wonderful along with the things that may seem painful or not so
enjoyable. Once your horse life becomes simply life, you can
start to feel the same about all of your rides.

*But I will never be Ray Hunt or Buck Brannaman.*

—sources too numerous to list!

This kind of lament can be heard by almost anyone who is trying to become a better horseman or horsewoman. I know for me it truly is not likely I will ever be anywhere near as good as either of these men or any of the other horsemen and horsewomen I admire. But that certainly doesn't stop me from aspiring to understand what they know and even if I can get just a little bit closer, my horses' lives and my horse life will be better than before.

*I must only warn you of one thing. You have become a
different person in the course of these years. Perhaps you
have hardly noticed it yet, but you will feel it strongly
when you meet your friends and acquaintances again in
your own country: things will no longer harmonize as
before. You will see with other eyes and measure with
other measures.*

—from *Zen in the Art of Archery*
by Eugen Herrigel

I was so surprised when I read this passage several years
ago—that what I was feeling after I went to my first Buck
Brannaman clinic was right there in print. I couldn't define it, I
couldn't put it into words, I certainly couldn't put it into practice, but I had clearly seen what I had long been looking for in
regard to having a relationship with horses.

I had known for a month or so that after the clinic, I would
need to move my horse out of the barn he had been in when I
bought him. I had found a tentative place but when the clinic
was over I felt I needed to move him to the facility where the
clinic took place. I could not understand or communicate (let
alone accomplish) what I had seen and I knew if I ended up
somewhere where no one had seen, heard, or followed this
approach I would be back on a slippery slope.

After numerous years of attending clinics and developing
some level of understanding of what I do consider to be simply
good horsemanship (a concept instilled in me by Greg Eliel), I

now find I am able to branch out and ride with people who don't share or haven't run across this approach. I have become comfortable enough in my own understanding, my own interpretation, and my own horsemanship practices that I can simply ride and not have to analyze every little aspect of my riding. However, I still occasionally come to a point where I feel I need to be particular about who I ride with. I think that happens when I come to a crossroads in my own horsemanship with something significant that I am trying to understand; maybe it's a point at which I could make a leap in my own progress and so I intuitively purify my interactions until that leap is made.

This topic could be a book in itself, but what has happened over the years is that instead of feeling badly that I have times when I can't communicate with certain horse friends, I have decided it's ok. I do my thing and when I'm ready I can once again stretch my comfort zone. I thank them for letting me waffle back and forth, I thank myself for doing what I need to do to be true to my own feelings, and I thank my horses for not caring either way. They show their appreciation through their actions.

Ackerman, Sherry L. *Dressage in the Fourth Dimension.*

Allen, Woody. *Getting Even.* New York: Random House, 1978.

Atwood, Margaret. *Cat's Eye.* New York: Anchor, 1998.

Bacon, Richard. *The Forgotten Arts: Book Three.* Dublin, NH: Yankee Books, 1976.

Beckett, Oliver, Ed. *Horses and Movement: Drawings and Paintings by Lowes Dalbiac Louard.* London: J.A. Allen, 1988.

Bierce, Ambrose. *The Devil's Dictionary.* Oxford University Press, 1998.

Boone, J.Allen. *Kinship with All Life.* San Francisco: Harper, 1954.

Brannaman, Buck with William Reynolds. *The Faraway Horses: The Adventures and Wisdom of One of America's Most Renowned Horsemen.* New York: The Lyons Press, 2001.

Breathnach, Sarah Ban and Michael Segall. *A Man's Journey to Simple Abundance.* New York: Scribner, 2000.

Brooke, Geoffrey. *Training Young Horses to Jump.*

Brown, J. Jackson Jr. *A Hero in Every Heart.* Thomas Nelson, 1996.

Budiansky, Stephen. *The Nature of Horses: Exploring Equine Evolution, Intelligence, and Behavior.* New York: The Free Press, 1997.

Carroll, Lewis. *Through the Looking Glass.* New York: Signet Classics, 2000.

Connell, Ed. *Reinsman of the West: Bits and Bridles Volume II.* Hollywood, CA: Melvin Powers Wilshire Book Company, 1964.

Covey, Stephen R. *The 7 Habits of Highly Effective People.* New York: Simon and Schuster, 1989.

Dahl, Michael. *The Everything Kids' Joke Book.* Avon, MA: Adams Media, 2001.

D'Endrody, Lt. Col. A.L. *Give Your Horse a Chance.* Pomfret, VT: Trafalgar Square, 1999.

Dorrance, Tom. *True Unity: Willing Communication Between Horse and Human.* Tuscarora, NV: Give-It-A-Go Press, 1987.

Edgette, Janet Sasson. *Heads Up!*

Ertz, Susan. *Anger in the Sky.*

Evans, Nicholas. *The Horse Whisperer.* New York: Delacorte, 1995.

Fournies, Ferdinand F. *Coaching for Improved Work Performance.* New York: McGraw-Hill, 1999.

Gambardo, Geoffrey. *An Academy for Grown Horsemen.*

Gandhi, M. K. and Narahari D. Parikh. *Bhagvadgita.* Greenleaf Books, 1984.

Gibran, Kahlil. *Spiritual Sayings of Kahlil Gibran.* New York: Bantam, 1962.

Gilbert, Roberta. *Connecting with Our Children.* New York: Wiley, 1999.

————. *Extraordinary Relationships.* New York: Wiley, 1992.

Goldberg, Natalie. *Wild Mind.* New York: Bantam, 1990.

Golden, Arthur. *Memoirs of a Geisha.* New York: Vintage, 1999.

Gordon-Watson, Mary. *The Handbook of Riding.*

*The Gospel According to Zen.* New York: New American Library, 1987.

Grandin, Temple. *Thinking in Pictures and other reports from my life with autism.* New York: Doubleday, 1995.

Hamilton, Jane. *A Map of the World.* New York: Anchor, 1999.

Hassler, Jill Keiser. *Beyond the Mirrors: The Study of the Mental and Spiritual Aspects of Horsemanship.* Quarryville, PA: Goals Unlimited Press, 1988.

Hedgpeth, Don. *They Rode Good Horses.* Quarter Horse Outfitters, 1990.

Herrigel, Eugen. *Zen in the Art of Archery.* New York: Vintage, 1971.

Hiam, Alex. *Making Horses Drink*. CA: Entrepreneur Press, 2002.

Hunt, Ray. *Think Harmony with Horses: An In-depth Study of Horse/Man Relationship*. Tuscarora, NV: Give-It-A-Go Press, 1978.

Jackson, Jaime. *The Natural Horse: Lessons from the Wild for Domestic Horse Care*. Flagstaff, AZ: Northland Publishing, 1992.

King, Lily. *The Pleasing Hour*. New York: Scribner, 2000.

Klinkenborg, Verlyn and Lindy Smith. *Straight West*. New York: The Lyons Press, 2000.

Kursinski, Anne with Miranda Lorraine. *Anne Kursinski's Riding and Jumping Clinic*. New York: Doubleday, 1995.

Langer, Ellen J. *Mindfulness*. Reading, MA: Addison-Wesley, 1989.

Leacock, Stephen. *Guido the Gimlet of Ghent*.

Lee, Bruce. *The Tao of Jeet Kune Do*. Black Belt Communications, 1993.

Lively, Lynn. *The Procrastinator's Guide to Success*. New York: McGraw-Hill, 1999.

Lyons, John and Sinclair Browning. *Lyons on Horses*. New York: Doubleday, 1991.

Mariechild, Diane. *Open Mind*. San Francisco: Harper San Francisco, 1995.

Masson, Jeffrey Moussaieff and Susan McCarthy. *When Elephants Weep*. Delta, 1996.

May, Jan. *Equus Caballus: On horses and handling*. London: J.A. Allen, 1995.

McCall, Dr. Im. *Influencing Horse Behavior: A Natural Approach to Training*. Loveland, CO: Alpine Publications, 1988.

McCarthy, Cormac. *Cities of the Plain*. New York: Knopf, 1998.

McGuane, Thomas. *Some Horses: Essays*. New York: The Lyons Press, 1999.

Milne, A.A. *The House at Pooh Corner*. New York: Puffin, 1992.

Mohan, A. G. *Yoga for Body, Breath, and Mind*. Sterling, 1995.

Muesler, Wilhelm. *Riding Logic*. New York: Arco, 1977.

Murdock, Mike. *101 Wisdom Keys*.

Nin, Anais. *The Diary of Anais Nin*. New York: Harvest Books, 1969.

Osborne, Walter D. and Patricia H. Johnson. *The Treasury of Horses*. Outlet, 1974.

Palmer, Jessica. *Sweet William*. New York: Pocket Books, 1995.

Pennell, Elizabeteh. *Self-Defense for Women: Techniques to Get You Home Safely*. Avon, MA: Adams Media, 2000.

Peters, Ellis. *Brother Cadfael's Penance*. Warner, 1996.

Podhajsky, Alois. *My Horses, My Teachers*. North Pomfret, VT: Trafalgar Square, 1997.

Pony Boy, GaWaNi. *Horse, Follow Closely: Native American Horsemanship*. Irvine,CA: Bowtie, 1998.

Rand, Ayn. *Atlas Shrugged*. New York: New American Library, 1957.

Rarey, J.S. *The Modern Art of Taming Wild Horses*. Bedford, MA: Applewood, 1856.

Rashid, Mark. *Considering the Horse: Tales of Problems Solved and Lessons Learned*. Boulder, CO: Johnson Books, 1993.

Rosen, Michael J. *Horse People*. New York: Artisan, 1998.

Runes, Dagobert. D. *Letters to My Teacher*. Philosophical Library, 1961.

Ryan, Pam Munoz. *Riding Freedom*. New York: Scholastic Paperbacks, 1999.

Schaeffer, Rachel. *Yoga for Your Spiritual Muscles*. Theosophical Publishing House, 1998.

Scott-Maxwell, Florida. *The Measure of My Days*. New York: Penguin USA, 2000.

Seunig, Waldemar. *Horsemanship*. New York: Doubleday, 1956.

Sewall, Anna. *Black Beauty*. Grammercy, 1998.

Shiller, Robert J. *Irrational Exuberance*. New York: Broadway Books, 2001.

Simmons, Philip. *Learning to Fall.* New York: Bantam Doubleday Dell, 2002.

St. James, Elaine. *Living the Simple Life.* New York: Hyperion, 1998.

Steffens, Lincoln. *The Autobiography of Lincoln Steffens.* New York: Harvest, 1968.

Stegner, Wallace. *Crossing to Safety.* New York: Modern Library, 2002.

Steinbeck, John. *The Red Pony.* 1945. New York: Penguin USA, 1993.

Strickland, Charlotte. *The Basics of Western Riding.*

Swift, Jonathan. *Gulliver's Travels.* New York: Penguin Classics, 1985.

Tart, Charles T. *Living the Mindful Life: A Handbook for living in the present moment.* Boston: Shambala, 1994.

Tellington-Jones, Linda. *Getting in Ttouch.* Pomfret, VT: Trafalgar Square, 2001.

Vonnegut, Kurt Jr. *Player Piano.* New York: Delta, 1999.

Wanless, Mary. *For the Good of the Horse.* Pomfret, VT: Trafalgar Square.

# INDEX

## A

Ackerman, 9/16
Adams, 8/28
Adler, 3/14
Akiko, 1/24
Allen, J., 12/1
Allen, W., 4/7
Angelou, 12/8
Asante, 12/14
Atwood, 10/16

## B

Bankhead, 11/15
Barry, 10/24
Batt, 12/9
Beckett, 5/5
Bennett, 12/13
Berkus, 10/5
Bierce, 12/2
Bishop, 12/3
Blaine, 10/28
Boone, 7/26
Brannaman, 1/19, 3/10, 3/19,
    11/26
Brault, 8/21
Brooke, 8/10
Brothers, 8/14, 10/23
Brown, 2/17
Buddha, 1/4, 7/31, 12/7
Budiansky, 4/4, 8/1
Bulwer-Lytton 8/29
Burridge, 9/28
Burroughs, 10/20
Butler, 7/19

## C

Cainer, 1/11
Carnegie, 4/29
Carroll, 2/10
Churchill, 3/16, 7/1
Clarke, 5/22
Colton, 7/10
Confucius, 10/12
Connell, 1/30, 5/9, 7/11
Connors, 6/17
Cossman, 4/15
Covey, 2/26
Cox, 2/3
Crowe, 12/28
Cummings, 12/10
Curie, 5/15
Curtin, 1/12
Curtis, 12/15

## D

Dahl, 4/1, 9/13
Davis, 3/5
Dalai Lama, 2/9, 11/22
De Beauvior, 6/12
De Cervantes, 6/29
Demosthenes, 5/8
D'Endrody, 4/16
De Sales, 4/3
Dexter, 9/22
Disney, 6/16
Doctorow, 11/9
Dorrance, 1/27, 8/9, 9/25

## E

Ebner-Eschenbach, 6/8

Edgette, 4/2
Edison, 3/2, 10/22
Einstein, 10/26
Eliel, 9/23
Eliot, 6/13
Engels, 3/6
Engman, 11/17
Erhard, 5/14
Ertz, 6/10
Estrada, 11/16
Evans, 1/10

F
Ferroro, 12/12
Fields, 7/13
Fiore, 3/4
Ford, 5/1, 6/1
Fournies, 12/11
Frankl, 2/2
Freidman, B., 2/18
Friedman, M., 6/14
Fromm, 6/5
Frost, 3/31
Fuller, R.B., 4/13
Fuller, T., 6/18

G
Gandhi, 5/23, 8/26
Gambardo, 4/9
Gaugin, 8/18
Gibran, 6/20
Gilbert, 1/29, 12/4
Godwin, 9/8
Goethe, 5/19
Goldberg, 11/7
Golden, 7/2
Gordon-Watson, 4/23
Gore, 3/27
Gough, 7/8
Graham, 1/28

Grandin, 1/21, 2/7
Grant, 6/23
Gretzky, 8/23

H
Hamilton, G., 8/30
Hamilton, J., 4/25
Hanh, 1/15, 5/13
Harris, 3/21
Harrison, 5/24
Hassler, 1/2, 4/6
Hawking, 7/20
Hazlitt, 6/3
Hedgpeth, 8/17
Herrigel, 4/20, 12/31
Hiam, 12/17
Hill, 7/29
Hock, 2/14
Holland, 4/22
Howe, 7/27
Hubbard, 4/26
Humphrey, 5/2
Hunt, 4/17, 7/7, 11/20
Hurston, 6/24

I
Ian, 3/13
Ivey, 12/27
Iyer, 8/12

J
Jackson, 10/15
James, 12/5
Jefferson, 5/6
Jenkins, 12/23
Joel, 5/18
Johnson, 5/21
Jones, 4/28
Jong, 1/8, 5/17

K
Kafka, 7/4

Katz, 9/11
Keller, 1/25, 8/27
Kent, 7/28
King, L., 1/5
King, M.L., 5/28
Klinkenborg, 2/23, 6/7, 7/18, 9/4
Knight, 8/4
Koestenbaum, 12/20
Kozol, 7/15
Kursinski, 4/30

L

La Fontaine, 11/3
Langer, 4/11
Lao-tzu, 3/28, 10/25, 11/24
Leacock, 3/1
Leakey, 1/6
Lee, 2/4
Lessing, 10/4
Lewis, 11/29
Lincoln, 10/11
Lindbergh, 9/2
Lively, 3/24
Longfellow, 6/11, 6/30
Longworth, 7/24
Loren, 2/5
Lowell, 11/28, 12/18, 12/22
Lyons, 2/27

M

Magnusson, 5/27
Mariechild, 2/6
Maris, 8/11
Maslow, 10/8
Masson, 2/21
Maugham, 5/11, 5/16
May, 4/14, 9/18
McCall, 8/2, 10/6
McCarthy, 1/7
McDowell, 1/14, 2/25
McGuane, 8/31

McQueen, 1/31
Mencken, 3/3
Michelangelo, 3/23
Miller, 5/31
Milne, 3/22
Mohan, 8/16
Moore, 7/25, 9/7
Morris, 12/24
Mother Theresa, 1/9
Muesler, 8/15
Murdock, 4/24

N

Nelson, 5/30
Neubert, 11/1, 12/25
Nin, 11/27

O

Osborne, 10/7

P

Page, 5/20
Pauling, 11/25
Peale, 11/21
Peasley, 1/18
Pennell, 1/3
Peter, 1/20
Peters, 3/26
Picabia, 3/11
Pony Boy, 5/4
Podhajsky, 2/12, 4/21
Powell, 4/10
Previn, 11/10

Q

Quindlen, 4/19

R

Rand, 1/23
Rarey, 1/17
Rashid, 5/10, 9/12, 11/6
Riefenbaker, 10/14
Ringgold, 7/9

Roach, 7/17
Robbins, 6/4
Rogers, 9/21
Roosevelt, 9/5
Rukeyser, 9/1
Runes, 3/15
Ruskin, 8/18
Ryan, 6/15, 9/19

S
St. James, 8/7
Saki, 2/1
Santana, 11/26
Schaeffer, 8/13
Schwartz, D. 11/4
Schwartz, M., 9/9
Scott, 11/12
Scott-Maxwell, 7/12
Seligman, 11/11
Seunig, 3/29
Sewall, 2/22
Shakespeare, 7/3
Shaw, G.B., 9/20
Shaw, J., 9/17
Shedd, 2/13
Sheehy, 10/30
Shiller, 6/27
Simmons, 12/29
Simon, 11/13
Smiley, 2/8
Smith, E., 7/16
Smith, J.O., 7/14
Socrates, 5/26, 12/19
Soyer, 9/29
Sowell, 2/16
Spender, 3/17
Stegner, 11/14
Stein, 6/28
Steinbeck, 3/8
Sting, 10/29

Strickland, 8/8
Sulzberger, 11/8
Suzuki, 10/31
Sweeney, 12/16
Swift, 1/26, 6/22

T
Tagore, 10/27
Tangley, 6/26
Tart, 1/1, 5/7
Tellington-Jones, 3/22
Terry, 3/18
Thoreau, 6/21, 10/17
Thurber, 9/6
Twain, 3/9, 3/12

V
Vauvenargues 6/2
Voltaire, 7/5
Vonnegut, 11/5

W
Wanless, 8/3
Ward, 8/20, 11/2
Warner, 3/20
Weinbaum, 12/21
West, 8/22
Whitney, 10/3, 11/18
Wilcox, 5/29
Wilde, 6/6
Williams, 9/30
Wilson, R.R., 3/25, 9/15
Wilson, W., 8/19
Wodehouse, 6/19
Wolter, 2/15, 4/5, 7/6, 8/5, 10/9
Woods, 2/11
Woodson, 12/26

X
Xenophon, 12/6